CW00522498

Old Ma

Everyday Life

*for Jan.
always there for
me . love and thanks
x always
xx
Sue

enjoy - you old witch !!!*

By Mhairi Simon   *xxx*

*I would like to dedicate this book to all the souls,
both human and animal, who have helped
to shape this life for me.*

Table of Contents

Acknowledgements

This book has been quite a journey for me and committing it to paper a cathartic experience. I would like to thank all the ancestors for their teaching and wisdom and all the good people who persuaded me to put my story out there. Thank you to everyone who read the drafts and gave me constructive feedback especially: Debbie, Mary, Cait and Jenifer. My thanks go to David Coltman for our 'Jackanory sessions' with the first few chapters that gave me confidence to keep going.

To my two youngest daughters who gave me space and peace to write I give a big hug, thanks and a promise to try and give them more of my attention. And most specially a big thanks to my loving husband Dave, my soul mate, who has nurtured me along this path.

I would also like to mention the wonderful work of JK Rowling for the Harry Potter series who bought the possibility of magic to everyone's door and the Rev. Gregorson Campbell for his work on magic in Scotland and the information about Thomas the Rhymer.

Also, to Maddie Harland and the Permaculture Magazine team and Rob Hopkins for his work in Transition Towns for all their ongoing inspiration, I give my gratitude.

Last but not least, I would like to acknowledge my dear friend Guy Chalkley for his cover design and I will be pleased if my book can be judged by its cover!

Thank you to Fiona and the team at Cross Publishing for making this a reality.

Introduction

Magic is a different way of doing things.

Much magic comes from the Universe, from the past. It is already here, waiting to be found and used: it does not need to be invented or improved. It is, however, mysterious - that is its nature. And that is the conundrum: how to find and use something inherently mysterious.

For many of us, this conundrum can almost stop our efforts to find it.

But I know I was born with magic - it came with my soul.

I use this gift every day.

I consider myself lucky to be able to do that for the benefit of many others, some human, some animal. But it has not always been so: my journey has had it's ups and downs. Magic has brought loss as well as gain, and pain as much as a sense of identity.

Many people I've met have journeyed as though magic was somewhere over the horizon, aeons away, almost alive and determined to evade capture. I would like to tell you about my journey, so that you may gain ideas and encouragement for your own personal path. My main point is that Old Magic is close-by, still relevant and very, very interesting.

This book is for those seeking explanation and understanding of a path which is calling to them. At the beginning of a journey, the fear of feeling different or even insane can stop you in your tracks. I hope to reassure you that you are neither mad nor alone on this path. To many this story may seem fanciful or exaggerated, but it is as true as I can make it. To some it may be unbelievable, but to others this may feel like a story so familiar it could be their own.

At the back of the book I offer exercises and inspirations for you to try, or to immerse yourself in, because I have been guided to offer them. May your journey be one of excitement and illumination, but mainly a safe and happy one.

Warrior

72 BC, Valley of the Ashes, Isle of Wight

I watched as the rain ran in rivulets down my cleavage and the inside of my naked thigh. The sky had hung heavy for days just leaking enough moisture to seep into the hearts of the bravest and dampen their fire. Water dripped off the dark grey mane of my mare and ran in darkening streaks down her shoulder. She shifted her weight, oblivious to the gathering fear and the gathering storm. She knew to save her energy, as I did, until it was really needed.

The smir cast the distant hills into grey nothing and the open moor before us ghosted anything solid into fearful shadows. The warriors grew impatient as they could not see the enemy and it was hard to keep the anger up without a foe to face. I thought "Their priests have done well to cast this screen".

I checked again, my shield was solid, my hand through the grip, the leather thongs wrapped round my wrist, snaking up my arm beside the red morphic horse tattooed on my forearm and thumb. My sword sat gently in my right hand, weighted evenly with the butt so it felt light as a feather, the mackerel markings in the dark metal proving the skill of the smith. It was made by my grandmother and laced with her magic - it would not fail me.

From my right a small brown streak darted towards me and landed with a flick and a bob on my mare's neck. The wren tipped his beady black eye towards me. "Hail, King of Birds - you bring me a message?" I asked. He looked deep into my soul, his courage warming mine and with another bob and flick of his tail he was gone into the bramble thicket.

The drumming started and at it's first heartbeat, a collective intake of breath as the gathered crowd felt the reality of us being there. The young men and women roared their fight into the fog to release their tension and I watched as the elders exchanged glances and rechecked who was by their sides. A last loving glance was thrown in front of fear to family and lovers as the war band started to move downhill into the swirling grey.

My mare's warm damp hair rubbed against my thighs, her strength reassuring, the scent of her sweat soothing my churning gut. The drum beats following us grew faster and wilder as the first of the group reached the lower ground. Amidst the quickening music a solid beat of sword on shield was initiated by the older men and the roars of the young ceased. This was as it had been foretold round the fire.

Then it came - the inevitable stench of voided bowels as the mist revealed the dark mass of the enemy. Still and silent like a brooding demon they sat and waited on the other side of the valley... ... ...

Soul Magic

The Beginning

2010 AD Ashey Valley, Isle of Wight

The land as the winter hag lies still, her bone-bare trees pointing their branches to the early morning sky. Streaks of pink line the indigo dawn and the lightening horizon. Even in this naked state with her thorny briars and wilting grasses Mother Nature swells her presence in this silence. The ancient ash that squats by the burn stretches her bare arms through the clinging valley mist. She looks like a tree left over from Christmas as her brown keys droop in the damp air waiting for spring winds to send the seeds out on little helicopters to a waiting patch of soil.

The Sunday morning stillness is a time treasured, when the songs of the waking birds have peace to be heard. No rumble of the passenger ferry taking commuters on its twenty-minute sojourns to the mainland. No thrum of overhead planes decelerating to land in London, no traffic, no people - only Nature's sounds as she sighs and relaxes.

My dogs know this sigh as they lift their noses onto the breeze reading all the messages that it carries and tentatively they explore the start of the day. None of their usual terrier tussles, just a slow exploration of the lawn to discover who travelled this way in the night. My farmhouse sits at the top of the valley allowing me to look out over the neighbouring hills and down over the sea to Portsmouth. My land is an oasis of unspoilt beauty with ancient oaks, ashes, and alders but as far south as it is possible to be from my beginnings in Scotland.

Coffee in hand, I savour this magic moment. On the edge of my vision a small brown bird whirrs onto the windowsill to my left and announces his presence with a 'peep' too loud for his size. I stay very still, moving only my eyes to try to watch him without scaring him away. But boldly he flits onto the table by my side, bobs and flicks his tail. "Good morning King of Birds. Do you have a message for me?" I ask. My terriers break their vigil at the sound of my voice and dart toward me, making my messenger wren take flight to the safety of the nearby bramble. He lands and with a bob looks at me, head tilted sideways and I see the wisdom in his beady black eye.

My mind floats back my previous life as the warrior and her wren. The change in the valley now with the thick woodland cleared for farm fields and the valley mouth now holding the many houses that spill out onto the sea-front, holds no menace. Although still a beautiful area, man's expansion has scarred the land with fences and overhead electricity cables, but this morning's calm allows my mind to wander. It glides effortlessly in this stillness, glancing off other times, other lifes, times in this lifetime, and this journey.

Recognising Mine

For me, it began with a horse. She was a nine-year-old native pony - probably Dales breed - an unremarkable bay called Pal.

We lived in a small village in Scotland where my grandfather was a wealthy landowner and farmer. In time he died of alcoholism and the land was sold off for housing, but back then, it was still quite quaint. The train went through the middle of the village by way of a level-crossing, the rails protected only by a small cream picket fence, but it was still quiet enough to ride a pony through it - and for everyone to know everyone else who lived there. Many of the old religions believe that the soul reincarnates and lives many lifes on this Earth. This lifetime's journey came into my consciousness at the incredibly early age of one. My sister was 10 years older than me and she had riding lessons from a young local woman, who always hacked back to our house at the end of the lesson.

At one year old I was desperate to touch the horse and to sit on it, and regularly Carol, the teacher, would lift me to sit in front of her on Pal's neck. Like many of the country children I was encouraged to ride and to get used to being around animals. Occasionally I would be allowed to sit alone on the saddle and plod back to the stables as she cooled down from her ride, with only a supporting hand holding the back of my coat. And that's when it happened - my awakening!

I'm sure it happened by sense of smell - they say that's the first to stir in the body and the last to die. It is closely connected to the pituitary and pineal glands within the brain which have a lot of control and influence in stimulating the intuition or sixth sense. The smells of horse sweat, hair and leather wafted into my brain and suddenly I was *present*, as thinking and feeling and knowing as I am now 50 years later. I have memories before this, when I would see myself sitting in the big pram from outside of me. Or I would be aware of looking through the windows of my eyes. But this was the first stirring of being switched on and recognizing who I was. Don't get me wrong, it would still come and go - the awareness - but the knowing that I was housed in this new little person and that I *knew* horses from way before, was fired up in those early rides on Pal.

Memories stirred in me as this ancient soul looked out from the cocoon of a small person's body, to view the beginnings of a new journey. A sense of purpose was urging me to observe and learn and fulfil my role here in this life, but knowing what that role was had been lost somewhere in my transition into this baby. Sitting confidently astride this horse, soothed by the rhythm of her walking action, glimpses of other times flashed through my innocent mind and teased this soul awake even more. Even now as I sit in the garden I wonder how many people are aware of their beginnings. Doesn't everyone get an awakening as a baby? No, some tell me their wake-up moment happened later in life, others are still seeking an understanding.

ഇ⊙ങ

Children are children and I behaved no differently from any other child most of the time - demanding, crying, lost in my own selfish world of needs and learning and misbehaving - but when I was alone and playing, this was when my awareness was most alert.

Now, my mother was a busy woman, always worrying about something - anything, and usually nothing. Life was not easy for my family as my father had returned from the Second World War to find the family business in tatters due to my grandfather's drinking. Dad took it all on and moved into haulage with flatbed lorries and tippers. Stress took its toll on him too and he nursed an ailing business along amidst health worries which later were diagnosed as a brain tumour.

In the early sixties, children were not indulged the way they are now and I was told endlessly that children should be seen and not heard. Up early to my mother's rigid routine, washed, breakfasted and dressed in the best, then put out to play. Fashion and status within her social set was a large part of my mother's world and my birth ten years after my sister's was a huge inconvenience. I have never discovered if it was by accident or deliberate to produce a son to help my father or to try to mend a flaw in the relationship, but my birth has been shrouded in my mother's desire for outward perfection and the truth will never be known.

So my early formative years were spent largely alone with no other two-year-olds to play with, amusing myself in the large walled garden of the family home. Observation of nature filled my days and digging in the dirt I can view now was my early grounding exercise! I would toddle round looking at spiders making a web or watch how worm casts formed only to see the worm disappear back down the same hole. With all the time in the world I would become aware of where the birds repeatedly flew in and out with bits of grass and drawn to that place I would spy a newly-built nest. Eventually I would persuade my Dad to lift me up to peek in to see if there were any eggs. "Yes - one...two...five...seven!" I struggles to remember my numbers.

"So there are four eggs then. What colour are they?"

"Blue with dots!"

"Speckled eggs - they must belong to the blackbird"

"But it's a brown bird I've seen! And why are the eggs blue?"

"Mummy bird is brown and the daddy is black."

"But why?..."

My question was never answer as a furious blackbird swooped in, noisily protective of her nest. Dad and I both jumped at her shout and he told me it was time to leave her in peace.

The wonders of nature were a constant source of intrigue and mystery. Hidden beings of all sorts filled my garden hours and I began to witness the magic of life.

But my need for company stretched out to animals when no family were available to befriend me. I knew Pal - I had met her and when I awakened she *knew* me, so I would go to visit her and she would come to me. No not physically - I was a young child and enclosed in a walled garden and she was enclosed in her field - but I would travel out of body as easily as I could walk and spend time with her. Astral travel is always easier for children as they have no preconceived ideas or fears about what should happen - or could happen. I would just find a quiet comfortable place, usually on the grass behind the garage and go... It was my freedom and joy to be with her again and she recognised and accepted my visits with normal regard and mild disinterest. My mother however was a different story. "What have you been doing?" I would be asked - always asked. And when I replied that I had been to visit Pal the initial "Oh that's nice" gradually changed over time to the scar on my soul of "Don't tell lies".

Our house was always a busy house. My parents liked to entertain, there was always music, my mother on the telephone chatting to friends, some of my mother's social set liked to visit for coffee or my father was in and out from the yard behind the house to drink tea. Mum's noise was always just noise, like she needed to wrap it around her for security. Dad loved music and when he was not working he listened to Glenn Miller, Nat King Cole and the big band sounds and would dance with me standing on his feet. He worked hard but also liked to play hard. My sister, always my Mum's clone, stayed close to home hanging on my mother's every word.

So when not observing and enjoying the family dynamics of the four of us, when my Dad was at home, I would edge away to find the privacy of my own world either outside with my animal friends in nature or in my toy cupboard under the stairs. At first this suited everyone as I was out of the way, but increasingly being challenged and confused by the charge of telling lies, eventually I decided one day to prove the truth.

"Doggy Friend" was a big black Labrador who must have lived close by. He was a regular companion who would jump the garden wall and visit me behind the garage when called on the inner planes. By this I mean communicated with my mind. I had no training or instruction on how to do this, or even any conscious understanding that this is what I was doing, but when I wanted him to come I sat in my quiet place behind the garage and thought of him until a clear picture of him came to me in my mind's eye. Then I asked him to come to me. It was always such a joy when he bounded over the high wall and I would hug him and he would lick my face and wag his tail.

My mother had thought him an imaginary friend at first, but when I insisted he was real I would be told again "Don't tell lies or you will go to the burning fire!" Even at the age of two I remember thinking "Don't be so stupid, there's no such thing!". But the wise old soul within could not be heard through a child's lips.

So I decided to prove my truth by producing "Doggy Friend" for my mother to meet him. I called him in on the inner planes and when he arrived in the physical, I took him into the house. My mother was upstairs so I opened the fridge to give him a drink and keep him in the house until she came down. Her horror when she stepped into the kitchen to find me pouring milk straight from a bottle into the lapping mouth of a huge black dog, was beyond my understanding. I never did know if the horror was in the realisation that I was telling the truth, or that in her eyes a dirty, dangerous dog had violated her kitchen sanctuary.

Soul Purpose

I was told once that what we pretend to be when we are children is the key to our soul purpose. I found that hard to believe initially as all little boys would be train drivers or astronauts, but I started to examine my own past and things began to come back to me. Many hours spent alone in the garden amongst the flowers were making potions and medicines for the pretend animal patients in my pretend animal clinic. The things available to me were comfrey, rowan berries, sage and other things growing readily in the garden. Even then, an innate sense of what could be eaten, and what shouldn't be, was forefront of my understanding. Clearly I didn't understand what to do with them but it was certainly feeding my desire to heal and to serve. I can link this directly now to my practice of chiropractic for humans, veterinary chiropractic and the wide range of herbs and homeopathy we promote through my Natural Therapy Centre for Animals.

I have had many jobs throughout my life - dancer, groom, choreographer, teacher, bank clerk, life guard, bar tender, personal assistant - all while healing and doing hands-on treatment in the evenings. There has never been an obvious link, no career as such, they were usually just jobs that came up when I needed money. Now I can look back and reflect on the different life skills that they each taught me and have added to the repertoire presented in the more whole person now. Sometimes we can see no purpose for the jobs we take and can see no future in that work, but when we reflect back we can see that they taught an element of understanding that served us well in later years. The contentment that comes with the deep inner knowing that you are in the right place doing the right thing is difficult to explain - as many of the esoteric jewels are - and that is why in times gone by they were referred to as The Mysteries, taught only to initiates awakened and consciously on their path.

I am a server soul who's purpose is to serve, heal, teach and aid communication. I am a Gemini with strong links to Mercury, the ruler of communication, and this has had advantages and disadvantages on my journey. As a holder of the truth it was and still is quite difficult for me to convey what is obvious to me but may be unseen to others. Unable to lie as a child, my differentiation between spirit bodies, sendings (where the representation is out of body) and pretend friends was clear to me and easy to describe, but this caused fear and panic in my mother who dismissed it all as lies. My father would always tell me "With Truth as your sword you will win all battles" and that is a value I hold to today and will talk more about later. Naturally to protect myself, I would keep quiet about a lot of what I saw, both on the inner and outer planes or everyday life, for fear of ridicule. Not alone with this fear many with the same skills and knowledge would keep quiet and work covertly. This I guess is why many of the old teachings and earth-based religions have become so hidden that they have got lost and largely forgotten.

ഇ☉ര

My granny would often say I was "an old soul" - or that when I looked cross at something "I had the look of the ancestors". Recognising old souls is something I now do readily in both humans and animals. Many traditions separate humans by teaching that we have souls whilst animals do not, but this is something I disagree with. Animals have so much more than we give them credit for and I hope this will come through in my writing. The same granny would say "She's got the way with her" - 'the Old Way' being recognised in Scotland then as the old religion, or the land / earth-based goddess belief in which The Mysteries and magic were strong and commonplace. Herb-lore and tree-lore, animal communication and the second sight were everyday tools of the wise woman revered within her clan or village.

I was becoming more aware of my abilities with animals as I grew older. As a child of six I was beginning to see me as others saw me, not just in the singular presence and selfish thoughts of a baby. Carol, the lady who taught riding, had left the village and started teaching at an equitation centre eight miles away. Her horses, including Pal - my friend from babyhood - had gone with her as working liveries. Thankfully my mother indulged my desire to ride which also satisfied my need to visit my friend, and I rode there for a few years. My closeness and understanding of horses was becoming noticed and my skill at riding made me the star pupil. I was the student who was allowed to sit on the naughtier horses, or try the highest jump, or sit on the riding school's new purchases first. The innate knowing and inner understanding was quite naturally overlaid with the confident big-headedness of a young child!

My granny would often cut through my bravado and bring me down to size, grounding my ego. I would spend a lot of time at her house feeding chickens and pigeons and exploring the garden of her house. On wet days, like most little girls, I would explore her dressing table with crystal powder bowls, lipsticks, bowls with beads, rings and brooches. I would look in the mirrors which bent round enabling you to see the side and back of your head to ensure your hair was neatly styled. My mother and granny delighted in indulging the girlie side of this usual 'tomboy'. I was encouraged to brush my long hair with the silver-backed hairbrush and to try on some of the costume jewellery my granny owned. My memory of her is as a big woman but I know now that she was only about 5 foot 2 inches. She was a busty matronly shape but had a very big character. She was seen very much as a pillar of society and loved to socialise - I guess that's where my mother got the desire to do the same - but I grew to understand that in the background her knowledge of 'things hidden' must have been quite great.

The spare bedroom in her house had a high bed covered in some sort of animal skin backed by purple felt. I was fascinated and afraid of this room. A wooden door cloaked by a blue velvet curtain was the cupboard which held, in my mind, hidden treasure. It was always kept locked and my granny kept the key on a cord round her neck. On occasion she would open it whilst I was in the room and wafts of strange smells and unusual perfumes would delight my senses. But I was never allowed to look in.

Around age seven I was sitting one afternoon at granny's dressing table playing with a string of beads when in the mirror I could see my granny entering the room behind me. I knew she had been in the magical cupboard but I hadn't gone to try to snatch a glimpse of its contents. In her hand she held something covered with a blue velvet cloth which she pulled back to reveal a large crystal ball. I stretched out my hands to lift it but was forbidden, only to be told that one day it would be mine and when it was I would know what to do with it. At that point my mother came into the room. The furore that broke out between her and my granny caused me to retreat as my mother's words of fear shouted out "I have always tried to keep her away from this and now you're encouraging her". Having felt that I must have done something wrong I found the peace of the garden and sometime later was called in for tea, the whole incident forgotten and not spoken about again until many years later.

Soul Mates

In my Sunday morning garden the wren peeps loudly, dragging my thoughts back to the present. Effortlessly he weaves his way through the bottom of the hedge, appearing at a gap and checking that I am still watching.

Then he flits into the dark, out of sight, and I wait watching the gap for his reappearance... but he doesn't come. My mind drifts off again to a different childhood.

As a small child in another life, I was in Mesopotamia. This was revealed to me some years ago while I was being lead through a past life meditation by a skilled healer / teacher / friend. It also came as a bit of a shock. I was trying to make sense of some difficulties I was having in this lifetime focussing around material things like money and why I never have any, no matter how hard I work. Had this stemmed from a previous incarnation? Within the meditation she explored my relationship with other people and I recognised that I had always felt a little insecure and wanted to be liked. We revealed then that perhaps I would give too much away too cheap in business because I wanted to be liked and that my insecurity would have led me to fear that bartering for a fair price would make people walk away and go elsewhere. It all seemed logical, but where had this insecurity stemmed from?

Back we went within the meditation, tracking back in my memories thousands of years, back to a place where my consciousness stopped me. Suddenly a stark vision of a childhood in the times and place of Mesopotamia was in front to me. I was a young child wearing a loose robe of undyed linen and I was crouching in the mouth of an open dusty cave high on a hillside. In the shadow of the cave-mouth it was cool whilst outside the searing heat had baked the yellow soil. With me was a man in his thirties, dark, bearded, perhaps my father or my brother, he was anxious and he was hiding me here. I loved him and he was going to leave me but promised to return. I clung to him and didn't want him to go but he left. I waited. Flashing forward in time I saw me still waiting and eventually dying there. Sadness and joy struck me and I cried as I returned through time to the present. Sadness for a situation so real to me that my cells felt that pain embodied in me now. Joy because that man, although looking different now, is my husband. I could see immediately where my insecurities had stemmed from, especially in previous relationships when I might give too much in the hope of clinging on to a situation doomed to fail. I could see why the "love at first sight" relationship with my husband has always felt so comfortable and familiar. I could also tie in why I have been interested in the Jewish history in his family when my personal history is so far from that.

It had never occurred to me before that familiar souls in a father-child relationship in one lifetime may be lovers in another!

$$\text{℘} \odot \text{ℭ}$$

So my soul continues on its journey and this is the last time it will inhabit a body. The awareness of a final embodiment has grown on me gradually, beginning in childhood. The lessons that I have learned in my lifetime have been brutal on occasion and at the time it was hard to see anything good could possibly come from them. In retrospect, however, I can look it all over and understand how I have grown in character and wisdom from the various situations. When good things have happened I am able to rejoice consciously, thanking the universe for the experience. That consciousness is what enables me to examine myself, and objectively scrutinise my strengths and weaknesses and have the opportunity to work to improve things. The increasing rapidity in the lessons that have been presented, has alerted me to the process I am in. So now I can accept situations that are normally seen as life crises as stepping stones to enlightenment - God, that sounds evangelistic! But that is what I feel when I am able to accept a difficult situation and decipher its lessons and therefore find an amicable solution. My increasing understanding of this process is what lets me know it's my last trip. I am aware of many previous lives that I have lived, but I am only fully conscious of four, and this is another reason I feel this to be my last.

Past life stuff has always intrigued me but my knowledge on the subject is limited to my own experiences. Why is it that we hear of millions of people who think they were once Caesar, Boudica or Mary Magdalen? Why do we not hear about the man who was once Nobby Nomates, who picked his nose and drank beer, or fat Aggie who sold chips in a Glaswegian chip-shop? To me it feels like it is always the life of some super-hero, not ever an ordinary everyday no-one. My past life recognitions have come bit by bit throughout this life in glimpses, intuitions and dreams, and have gradually built a picture as layers of truth have been revealed.

Discerning what is truth and what is a passing dream is something that I have grown better at over time. It is being open to dowse that special ring of truth that resonates at quite a different level in your mind and body that makes you able to differentiate. The more occasions I have been confronted with past life stuff the more comfortable I have become with it and now I take the chances given to try to recognise soul-mates that I may have come across in the past. It is a time to try to get some little bits of the jigsaw into place and really begin to understand who we are and why we are what we are. I believe many of the people who come into our lives are people we have encountered previously - both good and bad.

We are all aware of strangers who we immediately resonate with and share the same values and humour, and we have that sense that we've always known them. Yet others we dislike for no good or obvious reason and again there is an underlying sense that we have known them before. Equally that sense of recognition can apply to a place when you feel you know it, have seen it or know something that has happened there before. Much has been written about reincarnation and re-embodiment, but for me this and mediumship is different from what I am describing. It is more a feeling that you have been there previously but you know physically in this life you have not.

An example of this piecing together of information came to what feels like a fuller picture, if not a conclusion, with one of my lives. As a child I had a vivid dream, one of these flashes where you can see, hear, smell and taste what is happening. You know, inside, what situation you have dipped into and although it may be very short glimpses, the realness of it shocks you and you awaken gasping, knowing that you have experienced a memory not a dream.

I was a warrior woman sitting astride a small, dark grey, hairy pony - I could see its head, ears and neck. Looking down I saw my legs were bare and I carried a shield and a sword. In the seconds that vision was with me I became aware of several things. The first was a striking red tattoo that looked like the Celtic morphic horse on my left thumb, and coiled dragon-like up my wrist and forearm. The second thing was that I was not holding any reins but guiding the horse with my legs. But as a child of seven I was still having riding lessons and the thought of going anywhere without holding reins was alien to me. The third was that I am left-handed and it felt odd that I would hold my sword in my right hand.

The same vision has come to me several times in the years that followed and each time I would glean a little more information. I grew aware that I was revered for my riding skills and ability to ride astride. This skill of riding and horsemanship links to my present ability with horses. It was many years later I was to learn that historically it was not unusual for women in this country to fight alongside the men and to wield a sword, but that it was more usual to drive ponies in a cart-like chariot and to jump off to fight on foot. I also became aware that I was not liked by my peers, but was respected as a vicious fighter. The sense that I was a bitter woman who had lost something was strong. I also became aware that a more senior or high-ranked woman was a love-rival but I never found out for who. Each time the dream would come, I could hear battle, smell blood, horse-sweat, acid from spilled guts, and see this red tattoo on my left thumb and forearm. And I was dreaming this before tattoos became fashionable on women! Although more pieces of this picture came to me about the warrior woman, I never did recognise her soul-mate.

The last time I had this dream was as a vision about three months before we came to the farm where we now live. I had looked at the farm longingly before we embarked on the purchase and we had thought it was called "Applemoor Farm". Still believing that was its name we came to view it and I was allowed to walk the fields and hedges downhill from the house, accompanied by the estate agent. With three-hundred year-old oaks and ash trees and ancient hedges, I was lost in the joy of nature when the dream struck me as a waking vision. It shocked me, and startled, I grasped at my left wrist, the site of the tattoo. Finding my composure I managed to pass off the incident without drawing attention to myself, but was left feeling odd and confused. My senses told me that this woman had walked these lands before and that I was meant to be here - I was being called back. But given that I hail from the north of Scotland it seems strange that I should have had a history in the South of England - all the same, the ring of truth that this connection was real convinced me.

We continued with the purchase of the farm and discovered it was called "Aldermoor Farm". I did not know much about the alder tree and could not find any on the farm, so I found a book and researched it's properties and tree-lore. Alder has also been known as "Bran's Tree" - Bran was a Celtic hero who instructed his followers that after his death his burial place was to be a powerful talisman of protection. It likes to grow on moist land, and we have three springs here, so that tied in. Then I reeled when I read that the catkins of the tree were used to make the red dye that ancient warriors painted themselves with prior to battle. It all tied in and felt like I had completed the puzzle - the last jigsaw piece in place. I'm back back on the land I have protected before.

ॐ☉ॐ

I could never share my visions or dreams with anyone because I expected to be scolded and accused of lying. Even at seven years old I was aware that some things should not be spoken about. However, occasionally something so magical and exciting would happen that I just had to share with someone and then it would be my granny I would turn to. She always listened with interest and without criticism. "Granny, there was a wee man behind the garage - I saw him hiding behind the old flowerpots by the hedge."

"Did he speak to you?"

"Yes - he told me where he came from and about all the beautiful things there and he played music on a pipe - and he wore really pretty clothes - and I asked about the animals there and he said they had horses and ..."

"Never, never eat anything he offers you - don't go with

29

him - and don't eat or drink anything with him ever, OK? That's how the fair folk spirit bairns away - pay heed to my words and don't take anything he gives you."

"Yes granny"

Subject changed, I would be distracted to another topic of interest but reassured that the magic I had witnessed was real enough to be concerned about. So I continued with my innocent explorations of nature, games of imagination and secretly practicing my ability to travel out of body. Life seemed wonderful and unchanging and the security around me seemed solid.

But during my seventh year granny dropped dead with a heart attack. My mother's life took a different direction as her closeness and dependency on her mother was shattered, and my life too began a big change.

Letting the Magic Flow

If magic is energy, then using it is about guiding it's flow rather than possessing it and squirreling it away. Some people seem to me to approach magic as though adding spells and charms and even gurus to their museum - sometimes a secret museum. My worry is that this leaves you weighed down with exhibits too precious to use or to let go of when you need to move on.

Doing What You Are Here To Do

The stages of Man are calculated in seven-year spans - a child is aged seven before it leaves its mother's aura. The second and third stages of my life brought a great many changes. The awareness was growing that I had a skill or a gift or a something that people were aware of and sometimes afraid of. I was still just me being me but could logically comprehend that if I had 'the second sight' or 'sixth sense' or 'old way', then I could use it. How I could use it, I didn't yet know and what this thing I had actually was, I didn't know.

How do you categorise something inherent and intangible? If I was an artist I would have a drawing to show, but being aware of and working with energy, healing and the ability to predict things is not something you can hang on a wall. To this day I still find it hard to label what to me is obvious, or to describe what I do.

This created a problem for a media team a few years ago who were filming me for a television programme. I had only agreed to do it if it focussed on my chiropractic work and if I could see the questions that would form the interview in advance. My senses were picking up that the journalist wanted to focus on the unseen and was edging towards the whacky entertainment market. The questions all appeared reasonable "What do you do that differs from veterinary practice?" etc, etc. On the day I checked we were working to the same agenda and the cameras began to roll. Suddenly each question was added to - completely changing its meaning - "What do you do that differs from veterinary practice, 'cos I've heard that you're a horse-whisperer?" I was stunned to silence then she said "Can you tell me - do you whisper to horses?". "Yes" I replied. The journalists' eyes glinted with pleasure and she moved forward with the microphone, signalling behind her for a close-up shot. "Can you tell us what you say to the sick horse?" she asked excitedly. I moved toward her smiling, mischief brewing in my mind and said quietly to her microphone "I usually say 'Get up you bugger, the knackerman's coming'"!! There the interview ended.

But what is it I do? Nothing unusual, I now know - something that most people can do if they tune into it. And so from age eight onwards my tuning in process continued.

My mother no longer had her own mother to support her, and she had dropped into the housewife role, organising my grandfather and his house. She was also becoming more aware of my father's failing health as his brain tumour was causing him to have epileptic fits regularly. That in turn began the demise of his business. In retrospect, this traumatic time did not leave much space for my mother to entertain a lively, intelligent child who asked awkward questions and did stuff that she felt difficult about anyway. But I was still delivered each week to the riding school and enjoyed visiting Pal, escaping into an environment where my skills at riding were appreciated.

As my eighth birthday approached I asked for a bike. I imagined myself streaking to freedom on a speeding,

32

shining, metallic steed - and hoped I could visit my friend from school who lived a couple of miles away. The second-hand, dumpy, heavy Raleigh ladies shopper was not quite my ideal, but it did give me my first taste of independence - and gave my mother space to deal with the ever-increasing stress she encountered.

Each spare moment I could, I would leap onto my bike to see my friend Kathy, and often we would go on another couple of miles from her house to visit my great-uncle's farm. This is when I became aware of the flow of magic that is available to us all and my skills at tuning into it started to surface.

My first conscious memory of 'the sight' being of use to me, happened on one of those bike-rides to Kathy's. From our village lanes I came to a stretch of long straight and fast B-roads. This was part of the rat-run between two main towns before motorways were built. My mother's fear insisted that I rode on the pavement to stay safe, and I would whizz along with the wind in my face, loving the ability to transport myself. An old hospital with a high stone wall lay on my left-hand side and curved with the pavement to a side-road. I would gather my speed and hurtle straight across the grass verge, leap off the kerb gathering enough momentum to cross the side-road and leap up the kerb on the other side, and on to Kathy's house.

One day on my usual journey, joy in my heart at escaping home and lost in thought, I started to gather speed for the side-road leap. A vision, so strong in my mind's eye, stopped me dead in my tracks, as I watched a red car speed from the side-road and onto the main road without stopping. Now feeling shocked and shaky, I got off my bike and I listened, but could hear nothing. The curve of the wall obscured my view down the side-road so I walked slowly and gingerly to the edge of the kerb and peered to my left. Suddenly a red car roared furiously in front of me, didn't stop at the T-junction and zoomed along the main-road towards the town. I stood very still, feeling sick and shaky - knowing that if I had done my usual leap trick I would have been killed - the car could not have stopped given the speed it was travelling at. I hadn't heard or seen it coming!

Often what comes naturally and is everyday in one's life does not seem unusual - how could it be - and so it is only acknowledgement and comment from outside that draws your attention to your own skill as being different or exceptional. This message had saved my life, and it woke me up to the possibilities the Universe offers us if we are open to listen and pay attention to them. Do you remember a time when opportunities have presented themselves but you have dismissed them as fancy, only to think later that "If only I had followed my instinct!"? Now I always pay heed to premonitions and sendings.

At the time I kept quiet about what had happened, not expecting to be believed. When the local paper reported the red car stolen, and the subsequent Police chase, my heart sank, and somehow I felt guilty. I 'knew' it was stolen by its behaviour, but I had no proof - so it was as though I was keeping two secrets...

೮໐⊙ର

So began the many journeys to the farm where my great uncle still kept to the old traditional way with horses as part of the workforce and small stone-walled fields, typical of the Scottish countryside. The farm lay in the foothills of a mountain range where most the year snow covered the tops like iced-buns and part of the land was given to a bog where the peat was cut commercially. Uncle Math had no children and so he and my Aunt Jessie welcomed me gladly and enjoyed having a child around

34

the place. I was also another pair of hands to help out, as the old farming methods were very labour-intensive, and even as a young child I was expected to work hard if I wanted to be fed at lunchtime, 3 o'clock tea or evening supper. My skills were soon recognised and Kathy would collect the eggs while I would be given things to heal - like half-dead chickens, cows that wouldn't milk or a wild horse to calm.

A local woman kept her horses at the farm, and one had become too naughty for her to ride, so my job was to sort him out so he could be sold. This was good, because now I could ride lots for free and so stopped visiting the equitation centre where my old friend Pal lived. My uncle's stables were magical to me as they had remained unchanged since God's donkey had lived there. Rows and rows of harness and head-collars hung on the wall, cobwebbed and dusty, with the exception of the five sets still used. The musty smell of hay, straw, horse dung and horse sweat was as comforting to me as the smell of new-baked bread, and it lives with me to this day. It brought back the memory from baby-hood of Pal's stable when she was walked home with me on board after my sister had ridden, and it was a special smell that I was to encounter again later in life.

I feel very privileged to have experienced the practical application of that old way of farming. There are lots of books and films and even television programmes these days which re-enact that lifestyle, but to have lived it - an age which was rapidly dying out round about me - has given me an insight and wisdom one can only truly understand by being immersed in it. The pace of life was definitely slower and this slowness is part of the secret to being able to tune in to the magic. Our lives now are all in the fast lane as a rule, as we struggle to keep down jobs, pay household bills, transport children from activity to activity and participate in the many sports, hobbies and pastimes we indulge in. All this in-between having spectacular holidays abroad!

This increasing modernisation began in the Sixties, when we were sold the belief that luxury was what we had to aspire to. Comparing that vision with what I watched happening on the farm drove me to question their choices. "Uncle Math, why do you walk all along this road cutting the hedge with shears - it takes you ages! Other farms use hedge-cutters on tractors, can't you borrow one?" I asked, thinking to myself 'and then I won't have to walk along behind him and pick up all those bits'. As usual he considered for a long time before he answered "Well now, I know this hedge very well - I've known it longer than I've known your Auntie Jessie. When I take time to cut it like this, I get to know where the wee birds nest and I get a wee peek at the spyugs looking gape-mouthed at me waiting to be fed. I see where the herbs grow underneath and I see a worn path where the fox uses it daily. I smell the wild honeysuckle as it begins to flower and if I take some home to Auntie Jessie it makes her smile and she might bake me a cake. And in the late summer I know where to find nuts that will give me a snack in the middle of the day. Do you think you would see all that or hear the birds sing if you were in a noisy tractor with a cutter going? But aye, I could believe your shoulder might not hurt at the end of the day." This gentle explanation and willingness to discuss, led me to find in me the ability to consider all sides of an argument and come to my own conclusion.

Although the world was changing fast, life on the farm seemed frozen in time - some said antiquated like the old men who still worked this way. Everyone else's desire was moving towards faster, quicker, sleeker, but on reflection not always better. The Sixties oil boom led us to an era of ready-made, use-and-throw-away and automation to 'save us time', like had never been known before. Instant fix for machinery and animals alike became the requirement and those who found all this change too much gravitated towards Math and his old-fashioned farm.

Where we lived, vets were not easily accessible and so most of the doctoring of animals had always been done by the old horse-men and plough-men, who's knowledge had been passed down for generations from man to boy. A group of men of varying ages would congregate in our yard on occasion and after much jolly banter would retreat into the stables, doors closed behind them with strict instructions not to be disturbed. I could never find out what this meeting was about although whispers of 'the horse-man's word' or 'Order of the Frog' occasionally leaked out. All I was sure of, was that you couldn't get the farrier for some while after, as his hangover lasted a good two days. Young men were initiated at a yearly ceremony, and the excitement and anticipation left its mark over the farm, but we female creatures were left out of the mysteries and celebrations.

ഇ⊙ൃ

Campbell the ploughman was one of these men. He was ancient and remained so in this timewarp. He would walk three-and-a-half miles to the farm from his home every morning and be at work, feed the horses, muck out and have them groomed, harnessed and everything ready to go before daylight. His routine never varied and I don't ever remember him having a day off. In farming that's not unusual as animals need to be fed and cleaned out every day - even Christmas Day - and so we have to do it if we keep them. The horses too were familiar with Campbell's routine, and this and his solid reliability gave them confidence and reassurance which they repaid with hard work and endurance. They knew their positions and would move un-led into place to be harnessed side-by-side, knowing where the other was in relation to themselves.

Campbell was deaf and dumb, but his communication with the horses was constant although mostly unseen and unheard, apart from the odd click or whistle. In these days before political correctness it was not unusual for us kids or even the odd adult to take the mickey out of him or mock his grunts in some way. At this he would fly into a violent rage, and it was not unknown for him to pick up a stick or pitchfork with the full intent of using it. But with the horses, dogs or cattle, never a hand was raised or anger shown, only gentle patience, consideration and care given at the same steady pace day in and day out.

Unchanged and unchanging, he presented at work in a tweed flat cap oily and greasy, his grey hair bushing out from underneath it. He wore a very white collarless shirt, always cleanly laundered, under a waistcoat and tweed jacket which had no buttons but was held shut in winter with a bit of garden twine or later baler twine tied around the waist. His tweed trousers of indiscriminate colour flew at half-mast revealing green hand-knitted socks and black leather boots. I learned later that the trousers were short by design and not accident, as it meant that they didn't get wet or muddy at the bottom when he walked in the plough furrow. Under his arm he always carried a rolled-up piece of sackcloth tied up with a bit of cord. We knew he carried his lunch in it, or his 'piece' as it was known at home, but what other treasures were within we never knew because he guarded it as possessively as an old lady does her hand-bag.

His gait was slow and considered with each foot carefully lifted and placed in line one in front of the other as if he was still walking in the furrow. He and the horses would work untiring at their steady pace, returning only as the light was going. Weary and dusty, the horses were washed off, their feet cleaned and brushed. They were strapped or wisped and then gently warmed under an old sackcloth or blanket. An appetising feed was put in their mangers as they returned to their stalls, thick with clean dry straw. There they were watched over as they ate, as Campbell wiped off the harness, oiled and prepared it for the next morning. Once finished eating, their water was topped up and clean hay put in the mangers, the now-damp cloths taken off their backs and a gentle brush given before the light was switched off. They were each given a clap on the neck before Campbell closed the door that ended a satisfying days' work and he began the three-an-a-half mile walk back home which he did at the same pace, down the now-dark country lanes to his village.

I only remember Campbell smiling twice in all the years I knew him. Once was when the horses were finally retired and turned away into the fields in springtime - a time when they previously would have been working their hardest. There were five huge Clydesdales and we took their headcollars off inside the gate. After a second's pause they all took off like the Grand National and careered over the fields, bucking and farting. The joy on Campbell's face as they did a lap of honour round us was reflected in the eyes of these grand beasts, their health gleaming from dappled coats. Poetry in motion they swung away again with fluid movement to gallop down the meadow, sun on their backs. We stood silent, the earth vibrating beneath us and watched through tear-filled eyes as they rolled and played.

The horses were replaced with tractors and our first red Nuffield tractor was given ceremoniously to Campbell. He was now so old that he came to work with a bike. He didn't ride it, but pushed it, his old gnarled hands on the handlebars, his sackcloth roll strapped on the parcel rack behind. He walked even slower, and the bike I think he used instead of a stick. I never saw him ride it, I'm not even sure he could, but once when he didn't know I was watching he stood on one pedal and free-wheeled down a hill. It made me smile to see him keek over his shoulder to see if he'd been caught. My father teased once that he was sure that Campbell got home in time to turn round and come back again. And so there was concern quite late one evening when my Mum and Dad came to collect me from my great aunt and uncle's farm when it was dark and we saw the light still on in the tractor shed. My parents rushed to the shed worried that something awful had happened to Campbell. There he was washing off the tractor and drying it with sackcloth - bedding it down for the night just like he had the horses! Old habits die hard.

The second time I saw him smile was some years later when most of the farm work had been taken over by contractors. Machinery was now commonplace on the farm and each year they got bigger and more automated. The young men, employees of the contractor, had little respect for the land and less time to listen to the advice of the old men. So when a tractor sank into the peatbog where they'd been told not to go, the task of extricating it became a problem as more heavy vehicles brought more water to the surface and the area was fast becoming a quagmire. Campbell watching this circus quietly, nodded to Uncle Math and they walked off to the field where the retired horses were. He and Math returned with a team of four hitched up and ready to work. Rising to the occasion, the Clydesdales sensed the tension in the air and jogged on the spot in expectation.

Silently Campbell moved them forward into position, the young men clearing the area, speechless at first, as he hitched the horses to the tow-chain attached to the bogged down tractor. Jibes and guffaws of derision were soon silenced by Uncle Maths roars and my claps of excitement as Campbell whistled the horses into action, and the chinks of chainwork taking up tension and the puffs and grunts of effort from the horses filled the air. The thuds of heavy hooves and powerful hocks as they dug in slowly pulling the tractor free of the mud, echoed the heartbeats of everyone watching, as with pride Campbell looked every one of these young men in the eye and smiled, white teeth gleaming through his grey beard, as he unhitched his four children and took them away to pamper them in thanks.

I often wondered how sore they must have felt next day, but there was never any sign of discomfort - Campbell's ministrations would have seen to that. Only once did I ever see one of the working horses unwell. This was unusual as injury and illness are common with working animals but I guess all mild complaints were dealt with immediately, so very little became serious. One of the horses had gone down with colic. This was rare then when horses were fed straight corn combinations tailored to their particular needs of the day and then worked hard enough to burn off excess proteins to prevent lactic acid build-up.

Treated for the condition, the horse failed to rally round and so free of pride, Campbell communicated to me that my healing skills were required, as he had tried everything his extensive experience could suggest. I still remember the respect he showed me - a young child - as he cleared everyone out of the stable and reverently stood guard by the door to allow me space and peace to conduct my treatment of his much-loved friend.

This gentle giant was lying sweating in his stall - pain racking his back and belly, an expression of fear in the dark pools of his eyes. His normally glossy mane looked dull, his dappled bay coat stained by patches of dark sweat. He couldn't get up. The danger was, that despite all the attention he'd been given, he may have a torsion - a twisted gut - and the only way to end it with dignity was to shoot him. We all felt this was not how this old horse should finish his days.

As I laid my hands on him he snorted acknowledgement and I went to work, allowing the energy to flow through me into him and start him relaxing. I let my focus drop to the next depth of concentration and called on the Universal Energy available to us all, to flow into me as I acted as a conduit, directing it to the areas of pain within this regal beast. His eyes widened, whites showing in fear and pain as things began to happen within him. His tail lifted and he strained as he gave a great groan and then he attempted to get up. I tried to keep my hands within his aura whilst trying to avoid his great thrashing feet as he threw himself back on the straw and rolled over. I had to keep drawing in this energy and feeding it to him - I could feel his pain - tears streaming down my face and retching with discomfort in my own gut - I held my focus, aware of Campbell's anxiety at the door as he watched the flailing efforts of his beloved horse.

After a few moments of heavy breathing the horse made a monumental effort to stand up and I stepped back out of his aura and waited. He lifted his tail and let go of an enormous fart and then with another great groan dunged. He looked at me for a moment then stuck his head in the hay like nothing had happened. Exhausted I leaned back against the wall of the stall and sobbed with relief. Suddenly I was grabbed into an enormous bear-hug from Campbell who also had been crying. He let me go with a respectful nod and went about settling the horse for the night. No more mention was made of the occasion at the farm as the job was complete.

It took me a little while to get over the event, and still does with those sorts of dramas, although I am better at it now. The depth of tuning in to the animal and aligning myself to its situation left me vulnerable to picking up on the negative energy that was causing or was created by the problem. I was in my teens before I became skilful at grounding myself and being able to hold my own space to allow me to walk away unscathed and undamaged, although it always touches my emotions.

ഇ☉ജ

One day when I was fourteen, I watched the men leaving from their guarded meeting as I swept the yard. It had been short and quiet without the usual raucous departure. Suddenly two of the organisers asked me to join them in the stables where the meeting had been. They said that they had talked about me and my 'ways'. It was considered that I had so much of 'the Old Way' with me that they had agreed that I should be given part of the initiation usually given to the young men. I felt afraid and apprehensive as they were so serious. They told me I was to promise never write any of this down and only to pass it on verbally to those worthy. They instructed me "Remember what you are being told".

This crude instruction is what I recognise now as the Hermetic teaching method of the ancient mystery schools of perhaps five thousand years ago. It stayed with me. I did not realise at the time what a special honour I was being given as I didn't receive the ceremony and celebration given to the boys. As a grown woman, now I can see how important it must have been for them to have broken long-standing tradition to have given this knowledge to a wee girl. I suppose changing times meant fewer were turning to these skills as vehicles were in general use and vets were taking over the treatment of animals with drugs and surgery. Giving this information to me meant many of the potions and treatments were passed on to be preserved. I still use them.

Gathering Skills

Many of the feats of magic and amazement are no more than good observation. Taking time to slowly get into the mind of the animal and think like him without letting our human brain get in the way is the secret. Then watch closely for what the problem really is.

I was lucky to be encouraged to slow down and look closely by living at the farm most of the time, absorbing the old skills and working at the pace of the old men. Regularly told to "Get off that bloody pony and do some work", I would resign myself to pleasure taking second place to getting the chores done. 'Riding-horses' were still seen as a luxury for gentry and real respect was only given to working horses. Many a time, however, I would provide entertainment by sitting on someone else's bucking bronco to the whoops and laughter of the old boys. Several times after one of these white-knuckle rides I would listen to the banter and the retelling of the scene, which they had found so funny, only to have it dismissed eventually with "Aye but you could see before she got on that he didn't like the cows, roll of pipe, sack on the fence, noise of the digger, etc, etc". So I began to look and truly observe what the horse was watching, feeling and thinking. It became a challenge to me to calm him down despite these things, because I had worked it out first.

This was how I came about my first event horse. A wild chestnut labelled unrideable had been brought to the farm for me to sort out. Calm when on the road, he became unholdable as soon as his feet touched grass, running blindly with no self-preservation. With no such thing as a sand-school to give me an enclosed space within which to work, I was encouraged to go to the nearby country estate. This big old house lay derelict, its grounds given back to nature, with the exception of the fields and an old walled garden, big enough to be planted out as a small cornfield and worked by Uncle Math. Now after the harvest, it was stubble surrounded by twelve-foot-high stone walls, it was the nearest thing I would ever get to a school. I entered through the large double gates made of wood which closed behind me to complete the rectangle of solid wall. The only exception was a pretty little wrought iron hand-gate on one of the long walls, the original entrance from a walk-way from the big house. Uncle Math and two of his friends stood leaning on this gate ready for the show.

I walked him round once, twice, and then eased into a trot. As we came round the corner of the short side this horse, called Rebel and aptly named, suddenly sat back on his hocks and broke into a flat-out gallop as if he had come out of the stalls at a race-course. Straight toward the solid wall he hurtled, then dropped his shoulder and changed direction. I stuck tight. Off again to the other side. Stopped dead, changed direction - I stuck tight. Flat out towards the third wall, dropped a shoulder and changed direction again to the cheers from the hand-gate. Totally out of my control he stopped opposite the hand-gate and eyed up the jeering onlookers who filled the only gap out of this place.

I sat there like the pom-pom on a bobble-hat, being wobbled about but hadn't yet dropped off. Then I felt his muscles bunch under me - No! He wouldn't take the gate? The gap was too small! The acceleration off his hocks must have pulled more G-force than a fighter pilot has to endure. We galloped towards the men who initially shouted and waved their arms as they had been doing for the last ten minutes. I watched his ears prick, lay flat then finally prick again as he jumped into the gap over the heads of the now cowering men, to freedom. I lay flat along his neck to avoid leaving my head on the stonework above and stuck with him as he made his way through the woods. I laughed with exhilaration and patted him as he pulled up. He had won his freedom and found me new respect from the audience.

Rebel and I had bonded as friends in adversity, and so we remained throughout our eventing career. My ability to stay on and my understanding of his quirky thinking was what sealed this partnership. Evil to most people who came near him he had gained a bit of a reputation, but some years later our bond proved unbreakable after a bad fall which knocked me unconscious. It was during a cross-country competition and a moment's distraction caused me to lose my seat and I landed heavily. I was so proud of my boy when I was told later that he stood over me and wouldn't let anyone near me. He would edge back towards me until his hind fetlock touched me and would snake his head back and forth, showing his teeth to anyone who approached. As he threatened to attack people moving towards him, decoys were trying to draw him away but each time he would realise and gently edge backwards until he touched me again. It took ambulance men, Police and officials over 45 minutes to come to my aid and only when someone had the sense to blindfold him with a blanket and pull me away did he calm down. Three days later Auntie Jessie visited me in hospital and let slip that she was glad to see me better, mainly because "That bloody mad horse hasn't stopped neighing since it was shut up in the loose-box when they brought him back". When I next visited he was as glad to see me as I was to see him.

The same skills of observation served me well in Ireland when I was summoned to sort out "a wee headache" in a top stud yard. Their best stallion would not cover a mare in for service and his diary was booked very tight. He must have a back problem they thought, and as I had sorted horses for them before they called me back in. I watched him cover a bay mare in the morning without any problems but with the grey mare needing serviced, he was completely disinterested and refused to perform. They brought him out to her two more times. Each time he came out eager enough, only to find his ardour dampened when he saw her. I felt for this stunning grey mare, groomed and plaited she was like the fairy princess being rejected by the frog.

I saw the problem and called for the boss. "I can get your mare covered but I need to wait until the yard is quiet." I said "and I need Sharon to help me". Sharon was the only girl in this yard full of budding jockeys and she took lots of teasing and got little respect. "Why Sharon - is it a woman thing?" he asked "Something like that, oh and by the way, she will need a hundred pounds in her hand before we do it". "Oh God is it dangerous?" he asked, now suddenly quite happy to pass it over to the most dispensable member of the yard.

Horses settled for the evening and the yard manager off for his meal, I called Sharon and we headed for the stud yard. "Now you must swear never to tell a soul what we are going to do" I charged her. Looking scared she promised, asking awkwardly if this had anything to do with magic or witchcraft. "No," I replied. "He just hates grey mares," I laughed. She looked relieved and helped me to rug her up to present her to her would-be cover. Unfortunately he was not so daft and lifted her rug causing the equipment to droop. Sharon was feeling deflated.

Ever optimistic, I asked "Where is the hose?" Thinking I had lost my marbles she directed me to the wash-off area where we unrugged her and soaked her with water. Leaving her wet, I turned her out in the sand-school where she lay down and had a lovely roll both sides. She stood up and shook. "Da-dah!" I said as I pointed to the now-orange mare. "Bring the boy round..." Without hesitation he did the job fully with a big smile on his face. We washed dried and rugged the mare and put her back in her box. I reminded Sharon not to reveal what the problem was and we reported next morning that our mission was successful. Sharon had received her tip and I returned home with grateful thanks.

Some months later I got another call from the yard reporting that the problem had returned. They thought that he may have injured his back again. I asked to speak to Sharon and asked her if the mare was grey. "Yes, same thing" she coded back to me. "Do you have a girl who can help you?" I asked, then "Let me speak to the boss".

"They will each need a hundred pounds in their hands before it", I convinced him. Persuaded I had taught Sharon well enough he paid both girls who conducted the same 'treatment' that evening in secret and reported their success next morning. As far as I know they are still doing the same 'treatment' when required, unless the yard lads have clicked that the stallion doesn't like greys.

Discovering the Power

Magic has a power, which may be it's greatest attraction. But until you know what the power is, you can't begin to make use of it.

Teenage Tantrums

Moving into the third phase of my life felt like a time of insanity. A skinny wee thing, but physically strong, I was very body aware. Fit with riding, swimming, hockey and climbing that I did enthusiastically at school and also cycling at speed to the farm, sometimes twice a day, I was a bundle of energy. My body remained pre-pubescent and I sometimes thought I had flattened my boobs with jumping on and off ponies and that they would never grow. The feeling of fracture came as I was entering that period of questioning uncertainty that all young girls go through, whilst having this old wise maturity within that fought the erratic mood swings of puberty. Compared to my school-friends, whose interests lay with pop-idols and boys, my thoughts of environmental activism and observation of the countryside, wildlife and nature seemed out of place. Horses were still more important to me than boys where my only real interest in them was competitive.

When some girls at school raved about the most fanciable boy in the senior year and what a dream it would be to go out with him, I felt irritated at their immaturity. Knowing my skills of persuasion and the power of the sixth sense, I knew I could make him ask me out. It shames me to write this now and it shamed the old soul in me then, but the teenage tyrant just wanted to say

- "See, it's easy to go out with him and he's nothing special, so shut up and stop wittering." The old and mature part of my inner being always let me be courteous and respectful. I never deliberately hurt anyone - the old tenets of magic must have been buried deep and influenced and tempered my behaviour - but often I would initiate relationships because I could rather than because I wanted them. I always got my man and started to know my ability and my sexuality.

I was a bit of a hero to my peers. You can understand that someone slightly mysterious and detached who was very self-confident, did draw attention. I never spoke to anyone about my abilities except to three of my closest friends. My inner maturity made me the agony aunt to many of the girls who were going through their own teenage traumas and although I always counselled them gently, their problems often seemed trivial to me.

At home things grew increasingly difficult for me. I loved my Dad and his sense of humour, but his health was failing. Still not old enough to view him adult to adult, I could only put him on a pedestal and see what I thought attractive. Glimpses of situations where the Universal Hand would tap me on the shoulder and say "Remember this, it's important" come back to me now as snapshots of time, and I wish I could relive them and ask more and learn more.

℘ ⊙ ℆

Being the Laird, a land-owner, my paternal grandfather had hosted many of the travelling people when they were in our area. Distinctions in Scotland and Ireland between tinkers and gypsies/travellers were clear and the latter were always welcome visitors. From ancient times, travellers would visit bringing news from other parts of the country, selling animals and skills as they followed the Earth's cycles, moon and star cycles and the earth energies. Respected for their traditions and connections to the land, they were received with welcome and were given hospitality in return for their news. From clan times, the traditional Scottish welcome was customary and anything less generous would be reported to other clans as they moved on, so in general they were received well.

Locally, our area was one of the well-known stop-overs where many of the travellers met with their scattered relatives to celebrate Samhain, the Celtic New Year. In years gone by it had been a big 'Tryst', an animal fair, and lasted several weeks and gave names to many of the village areas, like Goats Corner and the Bull Ring. In my youth it had developed into the kind of fair where side-shows and rides were prevalent, but the older generations within the travellers still lived in the old-fashioned horse-drawn and some now car-drawn caravans.

With my Dad having taken over from my grandfather, he welcomed them, not so much now as Laird, as most of our lands had been sold off to generate capital to save the business, but as a haulage contractor who would deliver hardcore to put down on the common-land where they parked up. This allowed the heavier rides to sit level and the public to visit without wading in mud.

I would visit with my Dad before the official opening and from childhood I still remember him being welcomed by the travellers in the old way, as Laird. He in turn would welcome them to the land, and although no longer farming, would accept on behalf of the village, the blessings they gave of abundance and fertility for the land and its people. We would walk through the site where the young men were constructing the rides, overseen by older men with big bellies and wary gazes. We walked on through to the vans parked up behind the activity and there the very old men sat in groups chatting. The smell of tobacco weaved around them and their banter was gentle and welcoming. They still carried an air of respect and knowing, and we sat by their fire and drank tea with them. Occasionally one of the old women would sit and join the conversation, and I was aware of the men being careful of what they said when the women were present. I smiled inside my head at the thought that the women were really in charge, even though some of the men seemed brusque and scary.

As a five-year-old I can still see Dad hugging one of the bosomy gypsy ladies and flirting outrageously as he leant over to put a ping-pong ball in a goldfish bowl behind her back so I could win a goldfish in a bag. With good-natured banter and much laughter I walked away the proud owner of a little orange fish.

As a fourteen-year-old I was more interested to eye up the talent and watch the leather-clad boys swing on the outside of the waltzer cars to the latest sounds of the Beatles. So when I was told I had to go and speak to one of the old ladies in her big van, I was reluctant and wanted my Dad to come in with me. He declined and I warily entered this dark old van to see what I felt was a creepy old woman. She looked like the archetypal gypsy lady with big gold earrings and a scarf over her hair, now long and straight and grey. This was a thing none of the ladies of my granny's generation would have, as a neat curly perm was the fashion of the day and I had never seen grey hair that was long! Her dark skin was creased and her hands bedecked with gold. As she smiled I was aware of large gaps where many of her teeth were missing and I was trying hard to look into her eyes and not stare at her teeth! Her eyes were dark pools which examined my soul. I was given a drink without being asked if I wanted it and was pleasantly surprised it was Coke and not some witches brew. The van was crammed with things, many of them hanging overhead and the dim lamp and candle-light reflected off the copper and brass wares around the walls. Very little was said but she took both my hands and examined the palms as she smiled and nodded. Then to my horror pinched my chin between her forefinger and thumb and examined my teeth like a filly for sale. She brought her face very close to mine and now with very serious expression looked deep into my eyes. Whatever she saw there was obviously to her delight as she cackled a laugh, patted my cheek and indicated that the audience was over.

Just before I left she came close to me and hugged me close to her old bony body - a genuine, crushing embrace. Then she took my hand and kissed it gently. She looked again into my eyes and bowed reverently saying "My lady". I didn't understand what any of it was about, but as I returned to my Dad who was chatting to a group of men I was aware that they all avoided my gaze as they turned and walked quickly away. As I tried to tell Dad what had happened he gaily changed the subject and no more of the weird encounter was mentioned, except that just before we went back into the house he murmured "I wouldn't say any of this to your Mum".

There was no-one for me to share this with, or any of the other weird things in my life. Although most things were discussed with my friend Kathy, I already knew this sort of thing was outside her understanding. She would always listen as good friends do but could only offer a sympathetic flippancy as she understood less than me. It was beginning to feel lonely and my isolation from my Mum and my sister was growing at a time when I needed female support most.

Feeling misunderstood as most teenagers do, I would fly into furious tempers which would be fuelled by my sister's bleating and constant reporting of every word exchanged with her, to my Mum. The unleashing of fury triggered my energy and my powers - which I was not yet in full control of - and things would break - like glass and electrical appliances. Again my sister would whine "Mum she's doing it again" and my mother would fly into a fear-induced fury. At times like these I would take pleasure in predicting something that was going to happen to my sister - usually a falling out with one of her friends - and my mother would send me to my room branding me a liar. Crying tears of anger, the temptation to curse them would rise to the surface. Not just the sort of "I hate you" curse that teenagers do, but the sort of sophisticated effective curse that I somehow knew I had done before in another life. Again the old magical tenet of 'harming none' would forbid me, although never in this lifetime had I had that training. Where had it come from?

This was a time of swinging between fun and fury. One minute my mature words of wisdom found the admiration to boost a teenage ego. The next minute I would be lost in a tantrum of tears at loss of face and the injustices at home. This led me to spout words of hate and anger which with my energetic abilities behind them had power to hurt. Still, the true curses were kept at bay as I learned to stand in my own space and hold my own energy. My moans and gripes of teenage trauma were listened to at the farm with patience and interest, but all the while I was encouraged to talk these things out while engaging in a physically exhausting task like moving hay or bags of corn. As your energy saps so does your fury and I was unaware at the time what clever counsellors my uncle and aunt were. "It's always the same" I moaned as I was handed a pitch-fork. "She makes sarcastic remarks and criticises my friends and when I tell her to shut up she shouts "Mu-u-um!" and I get the blame." "What does she, your sister I mean, say about your friends?" Uncle Math asked as he nodded toward the deep-littered byre that always need emptying when the cattle go out at the end of the winter. He started forking the muck into a trailer and I did too as I continued to rant my tale, venting my rage into the dung.

"... and your mother takes her side? ...really?"

"She always does, it's not fair..." as the first trailer-load is ready for emptying. And as the floor cleared, so did my anger.

The glorious time of my innocence was passing as I grew towards puberty. Late at developing both physically and to the streetwise side of life, I bumbled on, enjoying the beautiful side of nature and the energy there. My naivety was a useful tool as its honesty gave power to my magic, but it left me vulnerable to the dynamics of friendships and relationships.

We youngsters began to form a little gang at the farm. Myself and a couple of girlfriends who rode the horses, a few young boys who came from the village to help at hay and harvest and farmers kids from nearby would gather together on occasions, and games of sardines, kiss-chase and strip poker in the hay became exciting pastimes. Being the youngest - and on reflection the daftest - I was unaware of the interest the older kids had in members of the opposite sex. To be caught and kissed was enough to make me run like the wind and cheating at cards was better than having to take my clothes off in front of a boy. It took years for me to understand that when I was sent in to get jam sandwiches and a bottle of juice for us all, it was not the sandwiches that were wanted. Time after time I would finish up what was left over, sharing it with the dog, totally confused as to why the older kids would make off with the clingfilm as soon I brought them out. Only when I came out one day with the sandwiches wrapped in tinfoil and berated for it, was it explained to me that clingfilm and a rubber band was the readily available equivalent to a condom! Horrified, I never asked for the sandwiches again.

Eventually I began to mature physically and had a very lively group of friends. When not at the farm and working with the horses, I was enjoying a very happy social life. Young farmers' dances and discos organised by the local Scout Group were the highlight of my entertainment. More often than not though, I was indulging in some sort of outdoor activity and the school mountaineering group took me away on trips to the life I loved. The group of friends I made there became friends for life and the adventures in the Scottish mountains suited my independence and ideals of self-sufficiency.

Expeditions to walk and climb on hills and mountains ranged from one day to two weeks long. I was taught about the rigours and disciplines and codes of conduct in the hills. On walks we met with a wide variety of people of all ages and it expanded our outlooks and knowledge of life. It also extended our knowledge of German beer as many European climbers would come to enjoy the beauty of the Scottish peaks and we would share warmth, food and stories in the mountain huts or round a camp fire. This kindled my sense of the old travellers and their way, and gave me a connection to history and the land of the clans.

The beauty and ferocity of the hills never let me forget the force of nature or the power of the Earth to change one's fortunes at any given moment. I learned to read the weather and to understand its quick changes in the high peaks. So we ventured into these glorious ancient Caledonian forests with reverence and walked to the edge of the living zones where grass and trees end, and the noise of wildlife is limited to the call of an osprey or soaring golden eagle. We scaled the granite faces which reminded me of the hard stony depth of power of the mountain, exhilarated that she granted us safe passage. Each trip held different challenges and offered up a variety of prizes in the form of views from a ledge or sightings of rare mountain creatures or physical obstacles overcome. One trip in particular taught me more about my inner feelings and truths, than most.

I walked from Blair Atholl through to Aviemore via the Cairngorms and the Lairig Ghru, carrying a forty pound rucksack and with three days to complete the journey. I started out with Douglas, a friend from school, on the gruelling hike. All started well with mild weather and sunshine and we looked set to meet up as planned with another group on the third day at Ryvoan, on the Aviemore side of the range. I was aware that this was going to be a test of physical endurance but at the start I had no idea that my mental and emotional abilities were going to be tested too. On trials like this where the mental and physical are tested, I think one really begins to see inside and know the person you are. When you are the only one you can depend on and you know you have to dig deep in your soul to find that little bit extra, it tests your character and you get to know what you are made of.

We were walking strongly and freely and had planned to be well into the mountain range before we made camp on the first night. Our aim was to stop in mountain huts as we had no tent with us. These huts are called bothies and are there as rescue shelters, and in summer weather would provide enough cover for us to stop overnight. The first big problem we had was that my friend Douglas is six foot three and I am five foot four, and our stride lengths were completely different. He had planned our route and timings based on his walking speed and he made it clear that if I didn't keep up we would be behind at the end of the day. Then the whole thing could take five days instead of three and our friends might get Mountain Rescue out thinking we were in trouble. Neither of us wanted the shame of that so, I pushed on hard under the weight of my pack.

Warm sunshine bathed us as we strode along beside the river on a well-made track out of the town and into the foothills. We passed many other walkers heading back to Blair Atholl and as we warmed up we envied their ability to end their walk in the pub with a cold beer. Leaving town becomes obvious when the background sounds of cars revving and people shouting greetings to each other begins to disappear. Silence starts to get noticeable and the noise of everyday life fades to a distant echo. A car engine starting in the distance is heard, rather than being part of the constant drone. When in these still places, I found myself beginning to resent the grating whirr of overhead planes and found them an intrusion on the tranquillity. Birdsong, bees and running water began to bathe our ears, broken only by the occasional screaming take-offs of alarmed grouse.

Further into the hills as we left the river, there were few surrounding trees and we were knee-high in heather, and the only tracks were those made by rabbit or deer. The bee sounds turned into the annoying whine of midges which bite the edges of your eyelids and in Scotland have been known to make a grown man cry. Already my body was toiling. Biting midges driving me wild with itching, the heat causing me to sweat into my pack making it heavier as the straps started to rub and blister my back, shoulders and hips. Heather seed falling down the backs of my boots created horrible big blisters on my hot tired feet. Exhausted I continued, my wee short legs having to goose-step my way over the knee-high heather as I was struggling to keep up with my fellow-walker.

After eight hours of this punishment, I was asking myself what the hell I was doing there. This was supposed to be fun. Douglas wanted to keep going and I was desperate to stop. In fact I wanted to go home, I had had enough and longed to be beamed up to a civilised place or find a car to drive me home. "Keep going" he encouraged, "The bothy is close by." Now I was beginning to observe what this body could and couldn't cope with, and feeling helpless, hopeless and tearful I continued like some spoilt brat toward the hut resenting every stride of discomfort that I took.

Arriving where the hut HAD been, we discovered some charred remains and a sign informing us that it had burned down in the last storm and the nearest hut was eight miles further on. I was bereft - sick, tired and miserable - my fortitude was being tested in a way no other test could. I had never before been in a place where I had to keep going. Most challenges are such that one can say "I've had enough now. I want to stop". But in the middle of a mountain range, with no roads and no-one to come along and take me home, it was all down to me. I plodded on, deep in my own thought, hating my companion for his height, speed and determination, and vowing never to mountain climb again, I was nearing the bottom of my reserves. After a while I was interested to observe my mental and emotional balance change as I moved from what I had thought was exhaustion to true exhaustion.

My griping, moaning, hate of discomfort had become angry, but now as the true physical failure was becoming reality, my courage and grit came to the fore and I began to drive myself forward. I was observing my emotions and reactions to all around me. As my temper flared, nature would provide a snag of heather root to trip me up and I got even angrier. As I sunk into a closed off place in my mind, a shadow of an eagle would cross my path and her loud call would cause me to lift my head and look despite my intention to stay depressed. Gradually as I tuned into the land I was covering and allowed my senses to drop deeper into my soul I could read the courses of energy on the mountain. Walking on these meridians of land-energy made travelling easier and fed back to me the energy my body was lacking.

We came to the next hut quite quickly and I moved into a mild euphoria which changed to elation as we pitched camp. I awoke early to peace, stillness and bright sunshine and repaired my broken body as best I could over the best breakfast in the world. That day I took my challenge on the chin, striding out in confidence even though the broken blisters rubbed. I ignored the pain and soaked up the surrounding beauty, the awe of the high peaks and the silence. I had broken me in - tamed something - I'd explored my true self in a challenge of spirit and I had come through it finding something in me that I hadn't known I possessed. I had grown. Douglas was amazed at the change in me as I took the lead and worked at a pace previously unknown. We made our deadline and met up with the other group. And I had found more than the joy of beauty - I had found another aspect of me and the new limits of my endurance and I celebrated them in the soaring heights of the mountain.

This place where we look inside and view our behaviour as a stranger might, is a place of transformation. Magic can only be performed when you know your own limits and can discern between your own emotions - what you create in your head by thought - and that which is external to you. Identifying that your own mind is creating a situation allows you to ground yourself and dispel those thoughts. Then you can pay heed to what is external to you and hold your own space.

Also, the understanding that by using your imagination to visualise what you want to create, forms the beginning of spell-casting and true magic.

Honing the Skills

As a teenager, my awareness of self-discovery merged with the general changes being surmounted on a daily basis. For me things felt doubly confusing - how could I balance the forthcoming challenges of adulthood with the deep wisdom I knew was housed in my soul. I became aware that I had something different because I could see that my friends and peers didn't have it. Sometimes I would say things about energy that I could feel or things that I could 'see' and would receive blank stares or questions of "How do you know this?". When friends were injured they grew to know that I could usually fix it with healing or manipulation or I would know the herb or homeopathic remedy for it. So I would be expected to do what I showed talent for, just as Kathy would be expected to play her piano if we needed music. I was also beginning to understand that I had to employ self-control to restrict my temper which could seem like a normal teenage flare-up, but all the time knowing that I had a power within that I could unleash to cause harm.

I had scared myself on a couple of occasions when fury overtook me and I vented my wrath, and only by seeing the fear reflected in another's eyes was I subdued. I once lost my temper with my paternal grandmother who was failing to understand what I was talking about. Despite many attempts to explain what I meant she seemed unwilling to grasp it. I felt cross at what I took to be her stupidity. I lost control of my emotions and felt my aura grow to enormous proportions. I could feel myself looking down on her and transmitting hateful energy in her direction. I felt changed into another being - perhaps what the ancients would describe as the embodiment of the Goddess Hecate or The Morrigan - I felt powerful and vengeful and angry. I wanted to open my arms and cast the stupidity I was faced with to the ends of the earth.

But then I saw my 'wee granny' step back in fear, she stumbled and fell down heavily on her bottom - she looked like I was about to strike her. Only then did I snap back into my own body and realise what I was doing. I remembered being told by the old men in the stables some years before that the power to heal has also the power to harm. Lifting my granny to her feet, she looked at me trembling and said "Please don't do whatever you just did again. Could you see yourself? - you changed and you frightened me". I felt ashamed and vowed to let the ancient voice of inner knowing guide me more clearly. It did very well and I opened my senses to this inner guidance and felt myself be more in control of my moods.

All worked well until a young man called Billy came to the farm and asked to keep his horse there. At first there seemed no problem and we rubbed along OK. Then I began to notice that he disliked me because I didn't fancy him or respond to his chat-up lines, and also because he resented the respect I was shown by Campbell and the old men at the farm. One day when I arrived to ride Rebel, my now competition-fit star, I was shocked to see that Billy had him saddled up and was riding him round the paddock. He was showing off to a girlfriend he had brought up with him and wanted to jump my horse and look impressive doing things that his own horse was not capable of. Rebel was being ridden badly and I could feel his distress. It had taken me years to get this horse to trust me enough to perform at his current level and I could see it being destroyed in front of my eyes.

Still in control I quietly asked Billy to pull up and get off as I had come to ride. He shouted some rough remark to me and kicked the horse hard while turning him sharply. Inside me I felt Rebel's fear and I communicated to him that it was OK to let it go. He did - he threw himself into a thrashing rodeo-bucking fit that dislodged his jockey immediately, and then walked quietly to me. I led him away to the stables.

Seconds later Billy was behind me swearing and cursing at me for making him look stupid. Still in quiet control I said "Never ride my horse again". I was still quite pleased at my ability to remain contained against such confrontation. I finished up my jobs leaving Rebel in his stable for the rest of the afternoon. I would return early in the evening to put him out in the field. Billy had gone off with his girlfriend to look at his own horse and I had considered the incident over.

When I returned at 7pm, I entered the stable block to hear Rebel snorting and stamping in distress. Fear immediately shot through me as I thought Billy might have come back and hurt my horse - something I had not considered. As I approached Rebel's box, I could see the whites of his eyes as he stared terrified at his bucket. I rushed into the stable to discover that his fear was caused by the kitten that Billy had just drowned in Rebel's water bucket and left floating on top for me to find. Billy's gloating face appeared in the doorway as I left the loose-box carrying the bucket containing this sad little corpse.

I still to this day do not know fully what followed. I do not know if I lifted the pitchfork in my hands or directed it with my energy but I became aware that I was willing it to hit this foul creature who was laughing at the distress he had caused. The fork flew through the air. The fear in his face as he looked into my eyes again brought me back to myself. The pitchfork sank deep into the hay an inch from Billy's head and he ran white-faced to his car never to return.

His horse was removed next day by his father who was very quiet, polite and clearly unnerved by the whole thing.

I was shaken and very upset by the incident. Strangely, it was one of the rare times that I explained it all to my mother with a full description of what I had done and it was one of the few occasions where she was fully supportive, appreciative and praising of me. Her love of animals was strong, although not always shown, but Billy's actions made her very angry. I don't remember her words but they gave acknowledgement to my power and she jokingly made reference to it being useful in this situation.

Again this glancing acknowledgement gave confirmation to me that something I was doing and something I possessed was real but unusual. I started to understand that you need this outer recognition of an ability to confirm something otherwise you might think it a strange quirk to hide and be ashamed of. I think this is how many people lose their natural skills that they have used through childhood, when they reach adulthood. Magic is difficult to describe, to understand and to come to terms with and many people don't want to feel different or unusual. I had to come to terms with the fact that I knew I had the power to hurt, and that for some reason, thankfully, I had stopped short of using to its full potential.

ဆာ ⊙ ෬

Isolating me further from my family was my academic ability. Having moved to secondary school I had awakened to the knowledge out there that began to tease something in my brain into action. My experience of the village primary school was a blur of nothing but being locked inside me. I moved to another primary school in another village aged eight when things had been re-zoned, and I realised that everyone else in the class could read and I couldn't. With no help from home I began to play catch-up and was bright enough to hide my weaknesses, of which I was embarrassed. But secondary school was very different and there I was encouraged by interested teachers. I wanted both their interest and teaching, and this propelled me into the top grades in all subjects. My interest in academia was met with my mother's mocking "Oh I suppose you'll be talking about University next" said with sneering impossibility.

Fun moved on to the more serious issue of exams and 'O'-Levels and Highers (the Scottish equivalents of 'A'-Levels) loomed in front of us, and the reality of life took its toll on our frivolity.

Being very academic I enjoyed the challenge of study but my mother disapproved. She saw my isolation with my books as unsociable and her fear became apparent again as she struggled to understand the subjects I worked on. Her ideal for me was to get a job in the local Post Office or follow her footsteps into the local bank. So when I was awarded a scholarship to read Physics at University, she did not allow it. My Physics mistress met with Mum, the Headmaster and me to plead my case. Sadly he felt that science was not for women who would eventually get married and have babies and advised that I listen to my mother. Distraught that my chance at quantum physics - which was my passion - had just disappeared, I found it hard to know what to do.

My intellectual horizons were broadening and my need to have questions answered was growing. Quantum physics was touching the scientific approach to energy that began to explain some of the stranger aspects of things I could do. Still I longed for greater knowledge and understanding of the esoteric and for a teacher to hone my skills and expand my abilities.

In America in the early Seventies, it was like the Wild West Medicine Show all over again with crystal shops and meditations on every corner. Scotland however was quite different as such things could still be viewed as Satanic and in the big cities, shops selling dream-catchers or Afghan coats were thought of as dirty hippie shops. My mother forbade me from going to them, for she feared I would bring back fleas!

What really fascinated me were the books that some of these shops sold which spoke about the things that I understood as normal. I would sneak in and read as much as I could before embarrassed into leaving and I would then have to roll about with animals so I would smell of shit rather than incense before going home.

The books began to offer explanations of how to meditate and reach deeper levels of understanding. They described auras and chakras, things that I had been feeling when I healed but had no names for. They also described the energies in nature with fancy colourful descriptions which made me smile. The old men had shown the same reverence but their descriptions were more earthy and real to me. At last as Flower Power was beginning to spread across the land, the world was beginning to talk my language - still not accepted as commonplace, but more readily available, and no longer did I feel quite so isolated.

Choices and Changes

Dad's brain surgery went badly and he was spending most of his time in hospital. My one ally at home was unable to help me any more and although so sad for his condition, my childish selfishness could only see me abandoned to the stupidity of my mother and sister. Dad had to close the business and although he did a little bit of work for a local company for a while, eventually he became unable to work at all. Money was very short and although my mother's father helped out a bit, the only way to survive was for my paternal grandmother to sell the family home and move in with us. That released enough money to clear some debts but day-to-day living was covered by Mum going back to work in the local bank. My sister, having left school with one 'O'-Level, secured a job there too as she was known to have come from a respectable family - that was the only credential required in those days.

Dad was dying and my feelings and emotions were still in a maelstrom and my dreams were evaporating fast. I found comfort with a boyfriend who offered a sympathetic ear and support. I also found closeness and love and the intimacy of sex with my now suddenly curvaceous body. Mentally mature and grounded now, it was easy for me to understand how I was viewed by older men since my body had changed shape and was attracting lots of attention. Still tuned in to the cycles of the moon and seasons and the forces of nature, I wore this body well but never abused its feminine capabilities. Sadly, no sooner had I found this new confidence than it was rocked when I was seventeen, when Dad eventually died.

Relieved of suffering and the indignity in which so many humans have to live out their final hours, he moved on. The family was for once united in our grief and gladness that his ordeal was finally over. When I went to see him when he was laid out, I found it very distressing. The body in front of me looked nothing like my Dad, even when he was ill. The funeral directors had done their best to make him look respectable but I thought he looked like the Sixties and Seventies hand-puppet "Lord Charles" as they had used make-up to give him some colour. I remember thinking 'what an undignified ending for so big a man'.

We are removed from death and its processes now as they have been handed wholesale to hospices, funeral directors and chapels of rest. When I was younger, granny was laid out in the best room prior to burial and the family could be with her. The best room in Scottish farmhouses was always cold as the fire was only lit on high days and holidays. I was saddened some years ago when a young patient of mine died of cancer and her mum wanted her home before the funeral. The body which had been bloated before she died oozed fluids as it decayed quickly in the centrally heated house and her poor mother had to have her removed again - all very distressing. The death process is very much a part of life and I think it is as important to die well as to live well. Perhaps a closer observation of death gives us more awareness of our own mortality and lets us value how precious life is. Only with that understanding can we appreciate the simple things in life and live with a more humble outlook.

Organised religion, in my opinion, nowadays conducts off-the-shelf services with little or no thought to the person or the family. The message given to Christians over many centuries is that ordinary man can only reach God through priests and ministers. This hands the power to the men of the cloth, relinquishing our responsibility for our own spiritual connection. So many of the mainstream religions have done this, dividing and separating the individual from Source, Universal Energy, God/Goddess connection and from the magic that life offers us. This has meant that for many, personal outpourings of grief have been contained and intimate comments about the deceased have been laundered into a dispassionate statement. I have heard many bereaved relatives say "I will feel better when we get the funeral out of the way". Brushing feelings under the carpet is not a way to celebrate a life lived.

Dad's funeral brought everyone from far and wide and I found the experience both sad and awesome as I realised the respect he commanded from those who's paths he'd crossed. When I was able to stand back and view this situation from a distance, I realised that an era had ended and I had to rethink what shape my future would take.

Having been sent off with a Christian funeral, I felt that I must acknowledge Dad's passing with the rites of 'the Old Way' and sang his soul on its journey to Source when quietly alone in the fields at the farm. Without having been taught how, I did what came instinctively and can see now that I was very close to the mark. The sentiments, being more important than the phraseology, did what was required and I knew that he had truly left me. Uncle Math was very caring and supportive through this period and although always checking I was OK, gave me the space and time I needed to recover my own emotions. The animals who were my constant friends were ever-loving and tolerant of me sobbing into their fur and always lifted my spirits. It was quite soon after this that Pal came back into my life.

૪૭ ⊙ ભ

Now competing regularly, or hunting with my own horses, my riding had moved up a gear. On Saturday mornings I had a young girl who came to help me muck out and look after the horses. The wheel had gone full circle and now I was the object of envy for my skills with horses as Carol, my sister's old riding teacher, had been for me years before.

This young girl rode regularly at the equitation centre where Pal lived and worked but she enjoyed helping me out in return for the occasional ride on my horses. Excited at passing on a bit of gossip, she came to my yard early one day desperate to tell me that at the riding school my old friend was to be put down. I replied sadly that I supposed that it was because she was getting so old, but she said "No, it's because she's vicious and no-one can touch her". Stunned, I asked her to unplait all the horses and turn them out as I would not be hunting but would be back in a while. I drove quickly to the riding school to find Pal. When I entered the yard I saw a group of children round the door of a loosebox where I could hear a distressed horse pacing and snorting. Derisive goads and jibes were being hurled at my old friend who was sweated to a lather and looking terrified in a corner. The new instructress was away in a sand-school teaching and unaware of how cruel the children were being. As one of the reliable horses for beginners, I could only guess that Pal had been over-used in the school and had just had enough. I asked where her tack was kept and was told that no-one could touch her.

I hadn't seen her for at least eight years and hoped she would remember me. "Come on old girl, you're going home" I said as I walked in to tack her up. She immediately recognised my voice and whickered a greeting, her eyes softening as she relaxed. I mounted and rode her out of the yard and headed for home and sanctuary. Next thing, a Police car pulled alongside me. "Madam is this your horse?" I was asked brusquely. "No, I'm stealing her" I replied "but I can tell you where I'm taking her and who she belongs to when I get home". Confused and not sure what to do, they drove off, leaving me to ride to the farm. On my return I put things right with Carol, Pal's owner who was in Spain and knew nothing about her being shot, and with the riding school who were happy to have got rid of her so easily. Pal was turned out with my youngsters and became nanny to them. I had my old friend back. She was twenty five years old when she came back and lived a long and happy life with me until she was thirty six.

I was becoming stronger and more at peace with myself. I was refining my talents at healing and I was more able to manoeuvre the energy that flowed through me. I could discern what messages the Universe was sending me but I was also shown that I had much more to learn when Pal reached the end of her life.

The changes came on her very quickly. From a glossy bright-eyed mare with the matriarchal attitude of control, we found her one day dull-coated and subdued. I brought her inside to the stables and we could almost see the weight drop off her before our eyes. My instinct was to make her better, heal her illness and soothe her discomfort. I became aware of Uncle Math's silence as I busied about her, thinking what to do. It still didn't click to me when he walked away wet-eyed that we were at the end. I had come up against death in other people's animals and the farm's animals, I had met it in my own Dad, but this was the first time I was to lose so close a friend - and one who I was responsible for.

I moved into position in her stall, ready to offer my healing energy and my loving friend turned her head and looked deep into my eyes. She communicated clearly that she loved me but needed no more healing - it was time for her to go. I was shocked and devastated - no not my wonderful girl - I couldn't bear another loss. Crying I rushed out and found Campbell in the yard. I threw myself into his arms and sobbed while he held me still. Unable to offer me words of comfort he waited, breathing slowly as I exhausted myself, then he tapped me on the shoulder. This was his usual signal for attention. He took my hand in his callused old leathery one and led me back inside to see Pal. Quietly he stroked her neck as I watched, thinking he had an answer. He did have an answer, but not the one I had hoped for. Slowly stroking over her back to her hind-quarters she relaxed under his hands then he lifted her tail to show me what I needed to understand. Blood and pusy discharge was oozing from every orifice. Pal was right, the time had come to let her go. Uncle Math made arrangements and the knackerman was to come that afternoon. On his arrival, I made myself scarce and awaited the dreaded bang.

I was still waiting when I felt that familiar tap on the shoulder - Campbell had come to find me. Pal wouldn't leave her stall and it would not have been possible to manoeuvre her carcass out easily, so I was needed to encourage her to take her final walk into the yard. I made myself strong and decided I must not show her my sadness. I clipped on the rope and kissed her as I always did and led her quietly out of the stables. She nudged me with gratitude, glad to be accompanied by one who loved her so much and I knew I had to stay with her to the end. Her actual death was very quick and over in the blink of an eye. She was freed of pain and the indignity of dying. If only I could have done the same for my Dad.

Again I found myself singing her soul home and releasing my grief in the quietness of the evening fields. Even the rooks seemed silent as they made their way home to their roosts. The world had lost a gentle soul who had brought love to so many people. I had learned that healing was not always about performing a miracle cure or even being a catalyst to recovery. Sometimes it's about easing the transition of the journey to the next world. A valuable lesson in humility.

Losing the Path

The watery sun casts a strange light into the garden. My dogs have settled at my feet looking quizzically at each other and back to me as if to ask "What is she doing? What's happening next?" They break my chain of thought and I smile to think how uncomplicated their lives seem. Food, fight, toilet, sleep, chase rabbits... more food! My head feels so full of clutter by comparison. Being human, with all the faults and failings that come with the condition, means that we can consider our own uncertainties as though they were a bad thing, rather than an opportunity.

Tasting Adulthood

Growing to understand my abilities, I now had to understand my losses and I began to realise that I was an adult. This sober time of my life had changed something and what had gone before had been lost forever. I had finished school and found responsibility, my childhood had gone and I was now thought of as a grown-up.

It had been made clear to me that University was not an option and I was expected to work and bring in some money. Submitting to my mother's will, I got a job in the local bank as a junior clerk.

This phase of my life was a time when I was least aware of magic and my connections tenuous, only appearing as passing glimpses. Having found a job, I became more aware of the value of money and material things. It was a time when I started to drive and buying my first car gave me the true freedom that my old Raleigh shopper bike had just fallen short of. My friends too were moving into their own futures and we were comparing pathways. Looking back now, it is clear to me that focussing on material things and moving into that mindset is a certain way to kill any connection with Universal Energy and old magic. Some of my peers moved away to University and I envied their choices and futures. Two joined the Armed Forces and escaped into new lives that way. A few stayed in the village and forged new businesses out of old country ways and continued the mechanisation of farming.

Those of us left in the village were the new young energy, the young earners within the community. We were the future of the village, the pioneers to forge a 'better' pathway of modernisation. Those who have stayed to this day made steady businesses and are still the pillars of the community. I have a fond memory from that time of Willie, a local farmer's son, who foresaw a future in machinery. He knew that the future of farming was in big pieces of equipment that would save time and the costs of labour. Knowing the reluctance to change that so many of the old men felt, he started a plant hire company. He hired out these big machines at decent rates and let many of those stuck in their ways taste speed and ease. Once tried, they would never again return to the back-breaking, time-consuming alternatives and so his business grew.

One day Willie got a call from an old boy who had hired a digger, and had got it stuck in a bog beside his remote hillside home. He asked if Willie could go and pull it out. Knowing he would need more hands, Willie asked another friend from our group to help him. Pete had a bad stammer which was worsened with stress and anxiety, but he was fondly known within the group as P-P-P-Petey, copying the advert at the time "P-P-P-Pick Up A Penguin". Willie knew the old farmer they were visiting was an eccentric old man who lived alone but was said to be one of the richest men in the area and so he courted the relationship. In Scotland, this old man's house was what would be called a 'howf' - unkept and basic - not reflective of the man's wealth. En route to rescue the digger, Willie instructed Petey that no matter what, "Say No" if he was offered a cup of tea. Petey gave a scathing glance, thinking Willie was being mean about paying for his time, and didn't enquire further why he should refuse. Shortly, they arrived at this barren hill-farm and found the door wide open - unusual in a hill-side home where a cold autumn wind might blow in - and were shocked by the resounding unmistakeable BOOM of a shotgun going off within the house. Fearing the worst, the two lads rushed inside to find the kitchen in chaos. Chairs were strewn aside, the table at an odd angle up against the sink and the dresser pulled away from the wall scattering the crockery onboard asunder. A second loud BANG as a shot echoed through the room made Willie and Petey dive for cover. A bearded face appeared from behind the dresser with cheeks as red as a skelped bum, the bushy eyebrows drawn in anger "Be with you in a minute boys, once I've dealt with this bloody rat!". When they dared keek behind the dresser there was the old boy with the double-barrelled shotgun down a rat hole in the floor. Shaking with relief that it was nothing worse they settled themselves on a kitchen chair as Angus pulled the furniture back into place. "Cup of tea, boys?"

"No thank you" Willie quickly replied.

"Petey?"

"N-n-n-n-nnnn..." Petey struggled as tea was poured into an old chipped china cup.

"Milk?" Angus asked brightly, still fired up after his rat-chase.

"N-n-nnnn-n-n-..." At that Angus gently kicked the cat away from a saucer of greasy, creamy, milk from which it had been lapping and lifted it to pour some into Petey's cup.

"There you go - now drink up lad, we've got work to do!"

Willie watched, choking back laughter as Petey grimaced and sipped at the disgusting brew. Angus, who didn't take milk, downed his and encouraged Petey to do the same.

After pulling the stuck digger free, Willie and the now slightly green Petey headed home. "I told you to say no to tea" reminded Willie. "I c-c-c-c-couldn't ge-ge-ge-get it out" stammered Petey. "I knew he only got milk for the cat" laughed Willie to a concise and articulate response of "Fuck Off!".

Many continued in this way, introducing new approaches to the old ways of village life and rapid changes redesigned the landscape. Some years later when I visited Uncle Math, when he had retired, I stood with him, looking over a gate to an area of three fields. They had been surrounded and divided by dry stone dykes but now as contractors were working the land with big machines they had been bull-dozed into one large field. We watched as they cut oats with a huge combine harvester at one end, rowed and baled the straw in the middle, and had the plough at the other end ready to dig up the stripped field to make it ready to replant. With tears in his eyes Uncle Math said "They're raping the land and doing a season's work in a weekend. She won't tolerate it you know". She was the land he had loved and caressed for his lifetime, and as I sit writing this in 2010, I think he was right.

A Time of Struggle

I struggled on in a brain-numbing, mindless job as I earned my first proper wage. With only my Mum, my grandmother and me at home, as my sister had got married and moved out, life had become boring for me. My mind was not being stretched and my social life was limited to horses, young farmer's dances and the occasional Hunt Ball. Although doing OK with my horses, competition no longer excited me and it seemed to be being taken over by the nouveau riche in their fancy lorries and very valuable horses. I was at an age when I was sensitive to being laughed at because I turned up looking like a 'hillbilly' in a cattle truck which was still plastered in cowshit.

I remember being at a big competition when I was on the receiving end of disapproving stares. My horse was the gleaming epitome of fitness and speed. Rebel was raring to go and was aware of the occasion as he strutted feeling two hands higher than his usual 15.3hh. In the collecting ring I chatted nervously to another girl who looked as terrified as me. Her own nerves kept her from analysing me.

"Oh no, you've forgotten your watch!" she gasped. I had noticed that all the riders wore large-faced, broad-strapped watches, which I thought were just a current fashionable adornment. As watches always go wonky on me due to my body's energy, I never bothered with them.

"Don't worry", I said - "I never wear one."

"Then how do you know how fast to go, and when to hurry up?" she asked curiously.

"By listening to his heartbeat and breathing, how else?" I asked, just as confused, as I stroked Rebel's neck.

She stared blankly at me and left me feeling at odds with everyone else on the field. It was only during my run that I observed what I actually did. So at one with my horse, I telepathically knew how his confidence and courage were. My ability to read his body language let me place him correctly at the jumps and guide him when any doubt set in. My knowledge of his pulse let me understand how tired he was and how much he had left to give, and his breathing let me appreciate what sort of pace we had been working at. The old men's teachings of slowing down and truly observing had given me insight into how the horse performs and I began to see the advantage of this old way of training a horse. My connection and knowledge of him had grown over many months of hard graft and I had an insight that a jockey who was handed the horse all prepared by their groom, could never understand. My energetic connection to my friend gave us a working partnership based on trust and devotion that is not commonly found, but remarkable when it is present.

Although recovering face when I would win, the joy of competition was leaving me and I was being drawn to a different lifestyle.

Changes in me were reflected back to me one day, when my horse had pulled a shoe off on a Thursday, two days before a competition. Jimmy Miller, who was my local blacksmith, a short fat man with a bald head and a flat cap, always wore his leather apron over a brown cowman's coat and did a fine job of shoeing my horses. Not one ever for the niceties of conversation, he was renowned as a grumpy old bugger and not someone to cross. Now adult, I had to make my own arrangements for shoeing and had called to plead with him to put the missing shoe on the Friday, before the competition on the Saturday.

With a gruff and grumpy response I was told there was no way it could be done so quickly. Disappointed, I resigned myself to the idea that I would have to miss this competition that I had considered might well be my last. Friday evening came and I prepared myself for the Young Farmers Ball, pouring myself into a low-necked, waist-hugging sparkly halter-neck gown, made up my face and styled my waist-length hair, feeling I might turn heads that night. The phone rang - it was Jimmy: "If you want that bloody horse shod, I'll do it now". "Fine, I'll be there in ten minutes" I responded, with hopes raised that I might ride my last competition after all.

I arrived in the yard all dolled up and under Jimmy's scrutinising gaze I took off my strappy sandals and pulled on my wellies, tucked my long dress into my knickers and pulled on an old dufflecoat and rushed off to catch the horse. When I brought him in I remembered Jimmy liked the feet to be immaculately clean so I deftly lifted a foot and began to pick out the mud, taking care not to scrape my nail-polish. Eyeing my cleavage, Jimmy's face flushed, "If you keep that up there'll be no shoes going on tonight!" Realising that I now presented as a curvy young woman, my tomboy ways were going to have to change.

Rebel's shoe was replaced that night and so were my strappy sparkly ones. My hands were washed under the yard tap and straw removed from my hair. The car wing-mirror was used to check the 'lippy' was still in place and nipples level in my dress. All OK, then off to the ball Cinderella!

I danced and flirted but used none of my energies to pull a date - it was all done on the sway of my hips that night. The handsome dark-haired lad with the pale blue eyes was the charming prince as he plied me with drink after drink, then I also swayed as I walked and he offered to take me home. I was still with it enough as I weaved to the car to hope I didn't smell of horse. As he held me and kissed me before we got in, his rough callused hands snagging on my dress, suggested as a land worker he might not notice. Inside his car the smell of cow over-powered even my perfume and we travelled home in silence as I struggled not to throw up.

The thumping headache next morning did not give me the competitive edge. My best boy, Rebel, took me as passenger that day and we managed a respectable fourth and confirmed to me that it was time to retire.

ഇ⊙ര

Change was happening all around and I decided I had to move out of my Mum's home because I needed to expand my horizons. I tried to get a flat in the local town, but Mum was very resistant. She had always needed people round her and didn't like the idea of me going away. Then one day I was invited to a student party in a flat in Glasgow belonging to a friend from school. He was Kathy's brother's friend and I had a bit of a fancy for him. So I went to the party taking my sleeping bag with the full intent of using it.

Circumstances overtook me - or rather too much red wine from the local Partick offy (which came in a lemonade bottle wrapped in brown paper, but it was cheap and effective) - and I stayed and moved into a relationship which on reflection was exciting but destructive. Built on my need to leave home, find love and security, and expand my brain, I started my new life in Glasgow.

The city offered parties, access to student life and friends with much to discuss. Every street had a pub, curry house and pizzeria, and the buzz and excitement of living in a place with joined-up shops and houses lured me from my country past. We lived in a tenement student flat that hosted many student parties, and we survived on my meagre bank pay and the remnants of a student grant. I was eventually transferred to a main city branch and romped through their grading system to reach the position of Accountant. My desire for stretching my brain lapped up the challenges of exams and the pay rises that came with each promotion but this furthering of my career was not to my mother's delight as I now outranked both her and my sister. My time in Glasgow indulged my need for laughter and I relished the quick wit of the local sense of humour. As time passed, it was decided that we should marry and after three years in the city, my husband-to-be had graduated.

The obvious move was to head back to the village where we bought a house, I changed jobs for a short while and then we started a family. All very grown-up and going what I thought of as smoothly, even beginning to meet my mother's requirements of a daughter - a nice house, professional husband - to all appearances an ideal couple. However, my husband who was under stress in a high pressure job began to change. Being adult and sensible didn't suit him and the constraints of providing for a family drove all the love out of our relationship. Over the period of the next eight years, things deteriorated and I was swept into a downward spiral of low self-esteem and oppression from an increasingly emotionally cruel husband.

It is hard for me now to look back on those years and describe how awful it was without negating the sense of growth and achievement that came from the hardship, and how good the occasional highs were.

I can now empathise with patients who talk about abuse outside or within marriages and understand the shame that most abuse victims carry. A lot of the time it is embarrassment at feeling so stupid as to have allowed it to happen to you and a sense of not understanding why you didn't act sooner to stop it.

In my case I feel ashamed to think that even with all my depth of understanding I couldn't see what was happening to me. I remember the pain of the constant fear - fear of upsetting the apple-cart - of doing something wrong. I remember the oppression of having to account for my every move because my car mileage would be taken to see if it tallied with where I said I had been. But it was not until my friend Kathy came to visit and witnessed me picking up the phone and just press the buttons randomly and replace the receiver that I began to wake up to myself. I explained that whenever my husband, who she also knew from childhood, came home, he would check the phone to find out who the last person I had called was! Then she listened to me being criticised for making a cup of tea below his required standard and she said "Vav, what the hell is wrong with you? Where has the feisty fighter gone?" I listened with surprise and had to examine my behaviour and admit that she was right. I had become a slave - a victim of abuse.

My husband knew my weaknesses as he had listened often to my upsets about my Mum and so he knew how to hurt me. He accused me of lying to him about who I had seen and where I had been. Finding some strength from Kathy's observation, I stated that if I was a liar then obviously I was insane, as he had previously accused, and I needed a psychiatrist. I then organised an appointment through my GP. The day came and I anxiously attended, not knowing what to expect, but Dad's reminder of "Truth as my sword" rang in my ears and I poured my heart out. The psychiatrist, one of the top in his field, seemed a pleasant and down-to-earth man. He listened to my whole story and asked various questions, which I answered fully, now enjoying the process of releasing all this bottled-up hurt. At the end of my two-hour session, he looked at me and smiled "You will be glad to know I don't think you're mad - in fact you're one of the sanest people I know. However, I have grave worries about your husband and would like to meet him." I knew my husband would never attend, but I spoke to him to give him the chance. My sanity was never questioned again.

The extremes of behaviour had become intolerable and in turn they were encouraging my behaviour to respond by acting in a way that my friends did not recognise. In fact the patterns of emotional intimidation were a more extreme form of the undermining I experienced at the hands of my mother and sister. This insidious form of control is clever because it leaves no outward signs of wounding, but searing insults cut into your very soul leaving you feeling depleted with very low self-esteem. Any time I showed new-found confidence, I was the victim of more accusations and I would be reeled back in to the maelstrom of madness, abuse and fear, trying to comply with his every need. Even the thoughts of cursing spells had been knocked out of me as I plodded through each day, numbed of my connection to Mother Earth.

I had been given reassurance that this problem was not mine. The psychiatrist had expressed his fears for my safety and I realised it was time to get out. At that time divorce in Scotland was still an unusual thing and this again would give my Mum reason to be ashamed of me.

The cruelty and emotional wounding of this experience I will leave behind here, but it did not pass in vain. I had learned a lot about me and this time the limits of my emotional endurance but now I had to call a halt to this sort of treatment and step back into the person I had been.

A Kick-start to Reawakening

One little spark of light during this difficult time arrived when I took a job as a personal assistant to a local potter. My job involved everything from organising import, export, exhibitions and throwing pots to cleaning the toilets. What interested me was that the pottery was situated in the old farm where Pal had been kept when I was a baby. On my first day I walked in to the now-refurbished farmyard where the display gallery was in the old byre and the potter's wheels in the old grainstore. It was explained to me that all the restoration work was done around trying to keep the original farm structure and fittings so that none of the character was lost. Then I was shown to my office where I stopped, rendered speechless with delight.

83

My office was in Pal's old stable, and my desk a piece of wood over her old manger. My silence was mis-interpreted as displeasure as many promises of upgrading to a better room were offered. "No this will do me perfectly", I replied, tears in my eyes as the faint remnants of familiar smells of horse, stable and my awakening wafted into my brain and kick-started my sense of independence again. It felt like whenever I needed her, my old friend could give me support, even when she had passed on so many years before.

After divorcing I was left with no security, no job, no home and only a small amount of money to put down as a deposit for a new home. I had escaped my previous life and my divorce went through quickly, but now I had to earn to pay a mortgage.

Free again to reconnect with nature, I put out to the Universe my need to find work. It had been so long since I had tapped into that energy that I feared that I may be spurned as a long-lost friend or punished for being so long out of touch. Very quickly my answer came when a local woman asked if I would help her sort out a problem horse. This was to re-launch my treatment of animals and led me back into a familiar world where I was confident to be myself and allow my magic to flow once more. I realised that the generosity of the Universe was not interested in the pettiness of human weaknesses and my request had been answered.

I moved south and found myself a place in a College to train as a chiropractor. This would give me a professional front to hide my healing behind. I met with an old-time chiropractor who saw something in my skills with animals, but as I was wary in this new area to let slip anything about magic, healing or energy-work, I let him believe I was just a good horse-woman. After watching me calm a difficult horse one day, he told me I needed to meet with some friends of his who would be interested in my skills. He felt they would be able to guide me in using my energy more openly. I was of course intrigued and now free to make a new life for myself, I was always keen to make new friends, especially those who may be able to teach me more about magic.

I visited the two elderly ladies who lived near the Rollright Stones in Oxfordshire and entered with trepidation to be vetted by them. I was immediately reminded of my visit to the gypsy caravan as a teenager. Able to allow that connection to influence my behaviour I courteously accepted their invitation to "do a little energy work", hoping to learn how to further my path. "So what do you know, dear?" I was asked. "Not very much" I naively replied. It was true, I didn't know very much - I didn't know the names of many of the things I sensed and I didn't understand my abilities or potential.

"Well dear, we'll just see what sort of energy you have and then we'll teach you how to project it", the dumpy one who smelled of lavender smiled. She asked me to sit on her dining room chair and ground myself "What do you mean, ground myself?" I asked. "Oh dear, dear", she responded, looking slightly mockingly over to her sister. "Never mind, we'll teach you how to do that in a minute - but first I'm going to approach you with this wand and just see what you're projecting". I sat still, containing my energy as she approached me with a copper wire with a crystal on the end. I watched as it bobbed gently as she scanned up and down my body. "It's OK dear, it's your energy that's making it move - that's OK, you have a good field - now let's see if you can make it move if I stand back over here - it's called expanding your aura". I allowed my energy field to stretch to her by the window and watched her crystal bob as I edged my field towards it.

By now I was enjoying this meeting where what I could do was not only understood, it was requested and respected. "Oh very good dear - when you get more skilled at it you will be able to push harder", she said. "You mean like this" I replied and let go of a blast of energy fired with enthusiasm. Like a laser beam I contacted the crystal which twanged back bending the copper wire. The sisters screamed and then giggled with girlish excitement. "I think we had better teach you a good grounding exercise, dear - this is a bit beyond us." And so they taught me a technique to ground my energy, one I still use today. I began to understand the terms to be able to describe what I'd been doing for years. At last I had found an opening to feel less isolated or unusual in my skills. These eccentric old biddies gave me a gift that I still value.

As I continued in my chiropractic training, my healing abilities proved very useful in assisting my assessment and as I progressed in my healing skills and energy work, chiropractic gave me an acceptable reason for people to reach me. I was rebuilding my life and relishing my freedom as it was the first time I had lived alone without my mother or husband, and I was loving it. My confidence grew as I was living with my magical Earth connection again, and I was safe in my own little house.

�begin{center}৪๐ ⊙ ৪☆

Time passed and I was growing as an individual and I was learning more about my abilities and opening up to Universal Energy. I was reading more about 'the Old Way' that was written about in many of the books I now had easy access to. I was a little disturbed to see much of what I did described as "witchcraft", as that was something that my mother had told me was a bad thing and was thought of badly in Scotland. The pennies were beginning to drop like wins on a fruit machine! "Ah, that's why my mother feared it" - the Old Way - the Way of the Wise - Wicca - Earth Worship - Paganism - the Way of the Sidhe - Faerie Folk and Faerie Ways. All these descriptions for the things that were natural to me were described in varying depths in books. But I began to feel that the magical bits were always left out. It was like I was reading a recipe book that describes a cake but doesn't tell you what the ingredients are. I would be left feeling that the book had missed the point.

I became more and more aware that many who were skilled journalists and poetic writers could pontificate a practice that they had never participated in. They knew very little about the substance of it. I was so lucky to have had my start in life to be able to know that so much of 'the Old Way' was rooted in old country practices built from the necessity of keeping your animals working and your family well. The old knowledge passed down through families about herbal potions or blacksmithing or animal skills *were* the Mysteries - the stories and songs and poems were how the unwritten ways were remembered. I felt honoured to have been educated with a hands-on skill which was witnessed and encouraged, recognised and nurtured, by the old ones of the country who still possessed the grounded understanding in the Earth Mother. This was all so far from what I would read about high magic with sophisticated rituals and priests and priestesses dressed in official robes.

The seventies were full of guru-worshippers and although it was sometimes difficult to remain confident on my own path when many encouraged me to follow this or that spiritual leader, I had been lucky to be able to discern authentic teachers who encouraged my journey. They could see where I was on my path, gently guiding me to my next point of learning. I was also fortunate to be shown by example how to slow down enough to *notice* magic - too often we are just too busy to be aware of it around us. I was learning the difference between ritual and ceremony, and recognising the theatrics of many supposed experts in magic.

During this time of recovery for me, honesty and self-awareness, elements highly valued in magic and 'the Old Way', allowed me to examine my own part in my marriage breakdown. Seeing that I had an involvement and accepting that I must take some responsibility for my part in it, helped me separate out what was not my doing. Distance from the situation allowed me to see honestly where and how things had gone wrong. Much became clear and my ability to connect to the rhythm of the land and the seasons helped me to slow my pace and work to correct old behaviour patterns in me that had contributed to my previous situation. I quickly became able to find the life-lesson that had been presented to me, I had learned from it and was able to move on.

Part of magic - and certainly of 'the Old Way' - is that forgiveness is important, and releasing bad feeling and not holding grudges is part of the healing process. If we take time to see our life journey as a spiral pathway we can understand that we will revisit a situation but on a slightly different level as we come round to it again. I was sure I didn't want to revisit this pain I had released and having worked hard with a relationship counsellor and my own inner journey, I was able to explore possible new relationships and even marriage in the future with a clearer vision of what I wanted. I was on my path again.

Expanding Learning

Growth and development usually come in fits and starts, often when we least expect it, sometimes when it is most inconvenient, triggered by new opportunities and slowed by pressures of life. While we might want to smooth out these ups and downs, perhaps some part of our learning is about taking them in our stride - finding wisdom in experience of life.

Wheel of the Year

Grounded back into the rhythm of the Earth I began to follow the seasons with renewed interest. The wheel of life according to the Celtic tradition begins in the dark times and like a germinating seed, grows and progresses towards the light. Samhain - 31st October - is the beginning of the New Year when the veils between our everyday life and the spirit world are thinnest. It is a time when many cultures the world over acknowledge their ancestors by celebrating the Day of the Dead. Nowadays we are plagued by the repulsive American 'game' of Trick or Treat, a bastardisation of an old traditional ritual.

As a child in Scotland I would go 'guising'. This was the time when all the children dressed up as a ghost or an old person - usually a dead relative - and carried a lantern made out of a turnip. Your 'tumshie heid' had a ghostly monster face when hollowed out and illuminated with a candle inside. In Scotland turnips are what in the South are known as swedes. So they were quite heavy and were held by making two holes where his ears would be and tying a string handle on. The lid was put back on top to keep the wind and rain from blowing the candle out.

The children would go from house to house doing a 'turn'. This was nothing to do with spinning round, but was the expression used for singing, dancing or orating a poem. In thanks, the grateful householder would put sweeties or fruit in your bag or pockets. The energy of this is that the child - a pre-pubescent virgin - was the pure and innocent bringer of the light, renewing the year and honouring those who had gone before.

The reality of it was that I was dreadfully embarrassed at singing in public and I remember once entering a neighbour's house with a little group of children from our area, feeling sick with fear and anxiety. When the string of my 'tumshie' caught fire from the candle it ignited the lid and sent stinking fumes of smouldering turnip up to blacken our neighbours ceiling.

The smell shot up my sensitive little nose and as I vomited all over our neighbours' living room carpet, to my friends serenade of "Weel May The Keel Row", the string of my lantern burned through and the whole thing fell to the floor, spilling hot wax and flames on both carpet and the child next to me. He screamed and the Collie dog in front of the fire jumped up and bit the child nearest to it.

Screams and now other retching children (because of the smell of my sick on the floor) were dropping flaming turnips and running outside whilst one stoical child continued to sing along with the old granny in the corner who was tapping time with her stick, oblivious to the madness erupting around her. The spirits of the dead certainly like a good laugh!

This leads us on to mid-winter and solstice - commonly the 21st of December, a time when we have the longest time of dark. It is in this darkness and stillness that we should take time to pause and think about the seeds we want to grow. The seeds of change, seeds of projects as well as seeds of plants, germinate at this time, and the dreams of what we want to see happen in the coming year have time to take shape. Having spent a fair time alone now, I was confident again in myself and I was enjoying dressing well and feeling slim and sexy. The power of the Earth was pulsing in me and I was relishing my femininity.

This time of creative thought is also a time of celebration when we can look back to summer solstice and see what we have achieved. The run-up to the more commonly celebrated festival of Christmas, I was seeing the fun of the forthcoming parties being a little less exciting because I was without a partner. I sat in the garden on a cold clear winter solstice eve, when the rest of the world was in bed or round warm fires, and slowed my breathing. I let the whirlwind of thoughts babbling through my mind ebb away and I asked the Universe "Am I ready for another relationship?". Quite clearly the answer came back "Not yet... but wait because soon the right person will come when you least expect it!". The answer contented my sense of anxiety and I was trusting being tuned into nature, so I anticipated my journey with joy.

$$\wp \odot \wp$$

The next festival of the year is Imbolc, which falls around the 1st and 2nd February and is a time of reawakening. The planted seeds are beginning to send out shoots and roots and there is movement under the dark earth. Although still cold and dark our patience with winter is failing and we are looking forward to brighter times. The projects we have formed in our minds are ready to go into the planning stage now and will move from being a vision to a reality. Having received an indication that I might be given a new relationship, I thought I should do some preparation work to find the right man and this was the season to start. The moon has always played a powerful role in the theatre of magic and is always associated with Women's Mysteries. So I decided to employ a little moon magic in progressing my path.

Like the cycle of the year, the time of increase and new beginnings is at the time of dark, so in the few days before the new moon I meditated on the shape of a new relationship. I opened myself to the opportunity on the inner planes that the person I would meet might be the right person for me and that our relationship might be a balanced and equal one. When a sliver of crescent moon showed on the horizon my meditations grew stronger and I started to name the qualities of the man I wanted to meet. By the waxing moon my vision grew stronger and at each meditation I lit a moon candle to help me hold the space. When the weather allowed it I would sit outside and commune with the growing face of Sister Moon. Just before she was a full round glowing ball in the sky, it was time to work my outgoing magic by sending my vision, hopes and dreams out to the ether and to allow her light to carry my thoughts through space and time. I asked the moon's blessings in finding the man who would be my soul-mate and someone I could share the rest of my life with. As she waned, I hoped my thoughts were travelling all over the world and visualised them being planted in my man's mind. Then I waited.

We moved towards spring, and it's equinox during the 20th to the 23rd March brought a little more balance. This is a time when day and night are equal, and the seeds have pushed their spring shoots through the soil to the growing light. Spring bulbs have grown and their developing flowers give us the hope that summer is again on its way. My chickens were beginning to lay and the Earth's fertility was showing as all her creatures were pairing again to breed.

With my hopes planted on the astral planes, I was free to focus on my chiropractic studies and was enjoying the hard work and friendships formed during that time. I was still working very hard to earn money and enjoying the horses that crossed my path for healing or to be worked with. With the end of the hunting season, many spring balls and parties were around and I was receiving lots of attention and invitations. Although flattered and enjoying the fun of it all, I knew that I had not yet met my soul-mate. So I concentrated on my house and my garden, finding the balance between doing and planning, inner thoughts and outer work and gradually my little house was taking shape.

When working in the garden my thoughts would drift back to Uncle Math's farm and the work that would normally be happening there at the time of my youth. After Aunt Jessie died, Uncle Math had virtually retired and the farm continued to be run by contractors. The changes in life were so overwhelming that he and many of the old men who had worked the land with horses, shrunk into the background feeling redundant because of the fast and complex machinery now in use. Chemicals replaced common-sense farming and speed was essential to make the land produce to its maximum.

At least I could work my small patch of garden organically using compost and horse manure as I had been shown. Working with my hands in the earth kept me grounded and connected, and I took joy in planting enough veg to see me through another year and cutting up dead wood for the coming winters' fires. As the last of the previous season's onions hung in the plait in my pantry, I watched as the young ones I had planted pushed and swelled to be this year's harvest.

Soon we arrived at Beltane, the May festival of fertility. My rows of potatoes were growing and my decorating almost complete, but no soul-mate had appeared yet. My friends were all keen to match-make and when we went out as a group I loved embracing the feminine aspect of life and celebrating my fertility by dressing sexily and feeling vibrant.

One evening I returned home to discover I had locked myself out. Dressed in my smart low-necked sweater, hip-hugging pencil skirt, stockings, suspenders and high-heeled court shoes, I felt slightly at a loss as to how to break into my house. Feeling a bit girlie, I thought I might ask my neighbour's husband if I could borrow his ladder, hoping secretly that he might rescue me. The only open window was my upstairs bedroom quarterlight at the back of the house. John next door, a local farmer's son and a bit of a lad with the ladies, gladly came to my rescue. His admiring glances of my sexy outfit were brushed off by both his wife and me as it was not meant to attract his attention.

Off he went up the ladder, glad to be my knight in shining armour, only to be confronted by my large German Shepherd dog who was not going to be convinced John was our friendly neighbour. Nothing else for it, I was going to have to climb the ladder. I kicked off my shoes and told John to cover his eyes as I hitched my tight skirt up over my hips. With John holding the ladder steady, I reminded him "Keep your eyes shut or you'll go blind!" as I began to climb. When I reached the window, a voice below chirped "Mhairi - I think I'll risk one eye!" and I looked down to a beaming smile and a mischievous wink. The stirrings of the season were making themselves known!

The year rolled on into summer and the solstice marked the longest day and the power of the light. Traditionally this was an important time when our ancestors would wait through the night to welcome the rising sun at dawn. Great revelry and parties would take place and feasts and dancing would mark the occasion. Growing things had reached their height and ripening started, giving us the abundance of vegetables, herbs and the start of fruit. I cut the grass with the sun on my arms, smelling the scent of new-cut hay and remembering the days at the farm when I would help to bring it in. It was a time of very hard, heavy and dusty work.

Hay bales from our area in Scotland were heavy with the rich soil and lush grasses. Uncle Math had made ricks when I was first a regular visitor. The rick was made in a metal basket, six foot across and eight foot deep, which the hay was thrown into and then trampled down and laid flat by a small person, occasionally me, who worked this cup of hay into a tight form. When full to the brim, a mechanism then flipped it over, at which point the small person had to leap clear as this dense mound of hay was plopped out like an enormous sandcastle and left to dry in the sun. The small person learned very quickly to throw arms outstretched so that when trapped underneath the suffocating mountain of hay, there would be something to grab to pull you clear.

With the baler, life was much easier but 'stooking' the bales into pyramids of three or five to let the air blow through and continuing the drying process, therefore preventing them sweating in the barn, was still hard work. The highlight was three-o'clock tea, when Aunt Jessie's famous jam sandwiches and a flask of watery tea was brought to the field for the workers. It was the most welcomed sight when you were tired and thirsty. I can smell it and taste it to this day! Everything stopped and the break was a time to rest and enjoy the companionship and camaraderie gained from sharing an exhausting job. The sense of urgency to make sure the hay was all in before the weather broke would encourage us to push beyond our tiredness. Often the idea of celebration at the end of the hay was lost to the need to rest and recuperate before the start of the corn harvest.

I sat in the garden with a glass of elderflower cordial, resting after my grass cutting, but I couldn't recover the same sense of satisfaction I had found at hay-time as a youth.

ೞ☉ಐ

I worked on through summer studying for my chiropractic exams. As July turned into August, we celebrated the festival of Lughnasad or Lammas. This is the time to give thanks for the harvest and was traditionally a time of fairs to trade wares and animals, the abundance from the summer's produce. Now with the grain harvest in, it would be a time to relax and celebrate. My celebrations then and to this day involve me meeting up with some friends who are also connected to magical work. Solo paths in energy work are always more challenging and can be more powerful, but the pleasure for me has always been in sharing knowledge and being with others who are on a similar path. I suppose just knowing that to others what I do is normal allowed me to feel included and part of a tradition, rather than ostracised and weird as I had been made to feel when I was younger.

Nowadays many festivals like the Goddess Festivals, Big Green Gatherings and Eco-Retreats are common and easily accessed places to gather with like-minded souls. They offer places to have fun and learn more about nature, Mother Earth and her Goddess aspect as the provider and carer of mankind. It excites me to hear the Mysteries taught openly to anyone who is interested and many authentic wisdoms are passed on.

Sadly, the openness of these things also encourages many deluded people, as well as frauds, who will trick the innocent by claiming they have power that can be bought at a price. So many self-taught priests and priestesses of made-up traditions declare themselves to be fountains of knowledge and High Magic, and teach invented rubbish to the untrained. This sort of practice dilutes the Truth and means that many with a true desire to learn are passing on mis-information.

Magic in its many forms is simple in its outward expression, the complexities experienced are on the inner planes. You will usually find that the true adepts are very ordinary-looking people who lack pointy hats and only offer their opinions on the Mysteries when it is requested from them, and even then they usually give it warily to those deemed ready to learn.

I moved towards the end of the Celtic year as autumn equinox and the end of September loomed. The seasons were changing, the garden beginning to change colour, the harvest of fruit coming to its conclusion, and my exams successfully over, but as yet the man of my dreams had not manifested. Like all practitioners of magic, I had moments of doubt, and I doubted my abilities and even its existence. This is a normal and healthy trait and is common amongst even the most accomplished. It is that little question in your head, usually at the most inopportune moment of a ritual or ceremony, that says "What on earth are you doing? Do you know you look and sound daft!" This is a good way to keep your ego in check as it allows you a moment to ask if you are still on the right track of authenticity and truth. Nowadays I smile when this happens and enjoy the visit from the 'trickster', a levelling face of magic.

Feeling happy with life and still open to the chance of a loving relationship, I put my doubts aside and continued on to my end-of-year lectures at the chiropractic college. Autumn equinox is another place of balance with day and night equal, and it was a time when I was feeling balanced in my life. I had released the past and was moving forward with clarity and hope. And there he was - a guest lecturer - the man of my visions - and I was dumbstruck. I sat in class examining his every movement, listening to his voice and scanning his energy field to see what I could glean about this stranger who had attracted my antennae. I had clearly attracted his too, as he kept looking at me as he spoke. My fellow students became aware of this electricity between us and I received lots of jibes at coffee time.

At lunch-time he invited me to join him for a pub lunch and quickly we found we shared a mutual balance in values and sense of humour.

Our first dinner-date led to an intense relationship that made us sure we couldn't be apart after only a few weeks.

Within a few months he became my husband, and we both had to accept that love at first sight is a possibility. My doubts were washed away and I was reassured that magic is very real. We are soul-mates and I know I have met his soul in a previous life. The circle was now complete, both in the year's turning and in my vision's arrival.

Moon Magic

I sat in the dark of the garden looking at the face of the moon. She had blessed my union and I had to give thanks. I looked at the glow and tried to see the pictures on this palette of silver. It is hard to believe that the light we see is only a reflection from the sun. That light, however, holds its own magic.

Our ancestors revered both the light of the sun and the light of the moon as they were aware that light was energy and therefore power. Many ancient stone circles are aligned for significant festivals to coincide with the sun rising and setting and for the journey of the moon. The ancient ones revered the hare, among other animals associated with the moon, as an auspicious animal who's image could be seen on her surface. Although I have always looked, opening my mind and allowing my vision to blur, examining all angles, I have never seen it.

The moon has a huge influence on Humankind and the other animals and plants who inhabit this planet. In magical lore she holds a special place and is strongly associated with female energy. The Earth travels round the Sun, but the Moon goes round the Earth, viewing her from all sides. The Sun's light on the Moon's face changes through the month as we see varying amounts of the illuminated part, altering her appearance to us. From full moon to full moon again takes roughly twenty-nine days and in magical lore the changing phases can be described as the Triple Goddess. The new moon is seen as the maiden, the full moon as mother, and the waning moon as the crone aspect of the Goddess.

Her journey round Earth creates a huge gravitational pull which affects the tide and all the water on the Earth's surface and includes that within the bodies of plants and animals. In humans, who are made up of approximately 70% water, with a brain of about 80% water, the effect on our mental state as well as our physical state alters as the moon progresses on her journey round Earth. Mood swings vary from happy through mild grumpiness and on to madness or 'lunacy'.

The female menstrual cycle of twenty-eight days culminates in a monthly bleed, often referred to as 'moon time' or 'moon blood'. It is well known by midwives that they are busier at full moon when a lot of babies are born.

Our ancestors would have used the moon's changes as a way of measuring time before clocks or calendars were readily available. History tells us that magical meetings were performed at the time of the full moon. This was perhaps because her energy was strongest, or maybe it was just that before street-lighting was available it was safer and easier to travel when you could see where you were going!

The changes in energy during the different phases of the moon allow us to use these changes to affect magical spells. For example, any wish for increase would best be conducted when the moon is waxing. Things like increasing bonds of friendship, or starting new relationships, building business, or bringing more money into your life. Or improving health and healing things would be the spells to conduct in the first quarter of the moon's cycle. Equally, any desire for decrease or reducing something would be performed on a waning moon - ending marriages, relationships or businesses. Outgoing magic would best be worked just before the moon is full to allow her light to carry it far and wide. Dark moon is a time of strong magic, closely connected to women's magic and was the time waited for by the cursers of old, as it is associated with access to the Underworld. All moon magic is best conducted outside, under a clear sky.

The moon was the original tool of the skryers who moved on to use a crystal ball. The ball symbolised the moon and could be used indoors in bad weather when the moon could not be seen. Traditionally, on a still night, the reflection of the Silver Goddess would be sought on the surface of a pond of still water. Sometimes a dark bowl full of water could be used, which could then be placed on an alter, or revealed from under a cloth to give more drama. The seer would focus on the light on the water and allow the vision to blur as the breathing slowed and the attention dropped to a trance-like state. Pictures, scenes and symbols would appear to the seer, allowing her to predict events or situations, or to locate a missing person. The moon-blessed water could then be consumed as part of the spell or used to anoint those present at a moon ritual.

For me, just knowing what stage of the moon cycle I am in keeps me connected to her magic and helps me to understand my feelings and moods of the moment.

Teachings Good and Bad

Living in the south of England introduced me to new energies in the land. It allowed me to sense the differences of grounding on chalk instead of granite. I also had more easy access to find different teachers with skills and things to teach me. Finding myself in a secure and happy relationship freed me to explore what I was comfortable with and gave me space to participate in many forms of work. Buddhism, faery lore, wicca, native American teachings and shamanism were becoming more common-place and experts - some genuine, some not - were more easily accessed. Each had something to teach me, but being secure in my original teachings and truths, I was not lured from my path.

The more I learned, the more I became aware of the commonality amongst traditions of spirituality. It served to make me want to root myself in my own ancestral traditions even more, and to learn more of the land-spirit-energy held in my genes from Northern Scotland and the lands of northern ice. But, seeing the spiritual traditions of other countries being borrowed for use in this country feels wrong deep inside. While they have allowed thinking outside the mainstream religions and have initiated many to explore what was once the old religion of this land, they have grown from a people whose ways and history are very different to ours.

Now confident in me - my history, my magic and my healing - my work reflected this strength and took on a deeper level of healing power. I felt able to promote my chiropractic practice with both humans and animals, knowing my skills to heal on the mechanical, emotional and medical level could be backed up with shamanistic-type healing and herbal knowledge. The 'Old Way' had given me a diagnostic tool more effective than most X-ray or MRI machines, but I use it quietly - though not exclusively - to find the best and quickest routes to health for my patients.

It was always so lovely, and still is, to have outside confirmation of what I intuitively know, and one wonderful example of this came to me several years ago in my chiropractic clinic.

My patient was a man in his mid-forties, best described as a big hairy biker. He was a gentle giant with a warm personality who happened to be a double amputee. Clinically, there are two sorts of amputees - elective and traumatic. The traumas are usually the result of an accident with machinery and the surgeons would do what they could to preserve as much of the limb as possible. The elective surgeries are done mostly on the elderly as a result of vascular disease. Then the amputation would be performed neatly at the best joint to form a good stump. Stump quality is important as it allows the easy fitting of an artificial limb or prosthesis.

My patient's stumps were not great quality, and were uneven, so I had initially presumed that they were of the trauma category, and I wrongly thought sustained in a motorbike accident, of which he had had several. Always accompanied by his wife to help with the removal and replacing of his artificial legs, we had established a trusting

102

relationship and would talk freely during the treatment. So when I asked on a check-up visit how he felt, he was able to confess "It may sound weird, but my feet ache." "No", I replied, "It doesn't sound weird - I have some experience with phantom limb pain" and continued to describe in a scientific way about neural patterning and the Kirlian photography with the phantom leaf effect that I had researched some years before. "Would you like me to try to relieve the pain by rebalancing the energy?" I asked, to a very sceptical and slightly distasteful look from his wife. "Anything is worth a try - it's driving me crazy" he said.

Now, with his prosthesis on, this man would stand at about 6 foot and 1 inch. He was a big built man, with quite a tummy, so when flat on his back he couldn't see what I was doing around his feet area - or where his feet should have been. This was where things felt different to other amputees I had worked with. Without his legs on, I was working in the area from the stumps to where the feet would have been, but I could not detect the energy on that line. What I picked up was that the left foot stopped quite a bit short of where the foot of a man so tall would normally be and hooked out to the left. The right foot stopped even shorter and the energy spiralled as it corkscrewed to the right at a strange angle. Trying not to sound surprised and thinking this must have been due to the trauma, I said "Your energy is spiralling here, I am just going to hold it still for a moment, OK?"

Not knowing what else to do, my instincts told me to still it just for a little while. I trusted my intuition, it had not failed me before. So without knowing fully why, I held on to the energy of his absent right foot. Suddenly he began to writhe about on the bench. "Are you OK - do you want me to stop?" I asked. "No, no, it's lovely, it's strange and a bit tickly" he replied, half-laughing, half-moaning.

His wife's eyes were on organ-stops as she watched this drama unfold before her. Able to see what appeared to be me holding fresh air and her husband in raptures, rolling about on the bench in front of her, and knowing that he could not see what I was doing, left her speechless. As things balanced and gentled, he relaxed and I explained that what I had found was an unusual flow of energy spiralling off in a corkscrew manner higher up the leg than where his feet would have been. "Oh no!", he said "That's where my feet were, and the way they twisted round - I was a thalidomide baby!".

I was left pleasantly reassured that my reading was accurate, and reminded that the old teachings were powerful and not to be forgotten. I was also reminded to be more thorough in my clinical history-taking in future.

ൟ⊙ඝ

Paying attention to the little things which occur in daily life often teaches us more than the many classes with so-called experts. Over many years I have searched for new teachings to expand my awareness. I am confident that we never complete our learning, so I am always keen to find out more and also to be inspired again. After such a long time of accepting my skills and helping others daily, it would feel uplifting and refreshing to further my development by having a teacher who could blow my mind by showing me something new. Many attempts at doing this have fallen short of my hopes, but have given me something to take away and develop, or have let me see things I already understand from a slightly different angle. This all adds to my continuing expansion. Sadly, other visits to workshops or classes have ended in less happy ways - some funny, some worrying.

A dear friend, who is quite an experienced soul along the enlightenment path, is a lady who loves to follow a guru and sees no wrong in any of their methods of teaching. Always kind enough to share her new belief system, she invited me to her latest teacher's class. It was being held in a large city centre in a huge venue and promised to be a powerful experience. Her partner, like myself, tended to be more discerning and we both read the flyers for this workshop with interest as it looked like it was based on sound teachings. Before the class began she introduced me to this Canadian teacher whose work was formed around building sound cathedrals and linking them to geometric patterns designed to energise a location with the vibration created. He was a pleasant well-informed gentleman, whose slight arrogance we excused as foreign enthusiasm.

Watching this hall fill with a variety of people, many of whom had no previous experience of energy work - one hundred and fifty people squeezing into place - awaiting our teacher's arrival in silent anticipation. From somewhere behind the scenes, a trumpet fanfare sounded and a grand entrance was performed by this man, dressed elaborately as an Egyptian priest, complete with makeup. Raising my eyes I saw my friend's partner biting the back of his hand to suppress his snorts of laughter and I immediately took a fit of the giggles. Always reminded as a child that the 'Old Ways' are never presented in solemn fashion, I found it hard then to view this ludicrous processional entrance with anything but laughter. Any credibility that the flyers had convinced me of, left me when he later failed to hold the energy of such a large group, and was totally unconcerned that many of his students left tearful and confused about the energy he had swirled about. It was a lovely lesson for me of how NOT to hold an energy workshop.

Yet, another time, I worked with two people with no experience in a medicine wheel led by an elderly Native American lady. The venue was a school in Sussex and the only area outside was on an asphalt playground, surrounded by a housing estate. Not conducive to the energies of nature, I thought, feeling disaster looming, only to be pleasantly surprised by the power of her ceremony and her care of the two ladies who had never done anything like this before. For me, it was a teaching in humility, as I walked round this playground banging a drum and chanting, watched over the fence by gob-smacked children from the nearby houses, but still a cone of power grew and was offered for earth healing and world peace.

So, often now, I long for the old people to be alive still, so that I can pick their brains, enjoy their company and find answers to my questions. It can feel very lonely without someone around to reassure me and offer their wisdom, and it can feel very daunting to realise that I am the old person now, moved into the crone role with the answers to other's questions. I still feel that I have much to learn but I fear that without the 'Old Ways' breathed into their life blood, the young people of today live without grounded foundation. This is a gap that I think will never close and maybe it is not meant to - perhaps a new way of being will evolve, different to the past and the present, but right for the world to come.

A Changing World

As I have grown and learned, so has the world - the old men at the farm wouldn't recognise it now. Some things are better, some are worse, and I feel that magic is more important now than it has ever been.

The Cloak of Illusion

I begin to realise now in my fifties that my true magic is held within me - not out there where I need to go to learn it at a cost. Uncle Math once told me, when I was feeling put down by a girl who pontificated about her horse's breeding lines and inferring that mine were of a lesser calibre, that 'empty barrels make the most noise'. Over many years I have seen the truth in this.

Only when I look round me at others whose skills I truly rate do I see that they, like me, seem ordinary people. They do not wear the façade of painted-on magic but quietly wear an invisible cloak of power recognised by fellow-wearers as such, and seen by the mainstream as a self-confidence which attracts attention. This quiet mantle resonates with a frequency of truth that leaves anyone coming into its path with a sense of trust and a belief of authenticity in that wearer. It comes in many forms and in all walks of life and the magic manifests in ways other than those normally perceived. The common denominator of these people is passion and integrity shown in how they conduct themselves and their businesses.

The true magicians are the people we see in run-of-the-mill businesses who refuse to be seduced by materialistic glitz and the desire for wealth. They run their companies, shops, training facilities, farms, publishers, garages, healing centres, vet practices, kennels, etc. etc. from a place of ethics with morals and codes of practice based on a desire to give a quality service or product. They have chosen their professions because they are passionate about their subjects and hold value in Truth. Sadly they are often the ones struggling to make a living because they will not compromise excellence for commercialism. Somehow, however, they survive and sustain, even through times of hardship and this is usually because they have a loyal and supportive clientele.

Business is an exchange of energy based on a fair price for a fair product or service. Balanced ethics in this allows commerce to succeed. Imbalance in the form of short-term profit may cause long-term damage to the purchaser, country or planet. For instance, rain-forest logging, over-fishing, pollution and total dependency on oil clearly make sense in one small commercial context at enormous cost to Mother Earth and her various inhabitants.

❧ ☉ ☙

I was once dammed by a business consultant. When I asked how this had come about, he said "It's the personal profile of you and your husband". "But if someone says I'm caring, generous and not at all ruthless, I take that as a compliment", I replied. "In business, it is one of the biggest insults I can give you", he apologetically responded.

"Then that type of business is not for me." I replied. My priorities were animal welfare and quality service performed by staff who were cared for and well compensated for their loyalty and hard dedicated work. I felt lonely and slightly stupid for being so proud and apparently useless at business.

I am not alone though. I have seen friends who will not be drawn into commercialism within their green publishing company when encouraged by marketing giants to jump on the eco-bandwagon. I know vets who refuse to become part of the current trend of selling as many drugs as possible to innocent animal owners before euthanizing their pets - they often have to operate without the security of a group practice to remain true to their beliefs that they are doing the job to help animals. And garage or pub owners who refuse to sell out to become franchisees of big conglomerates face the same dilemmas as little independent shop owners in that they struggle to purchase supplies at a decent rate. This means that places like supermarkets who purchase in bulk can sell to the public cheaper and therefore gain a monopoly on sales. Thank Goddess we are seeing a rise in the number of farm shops, farmer's markets and cooperatives holding on to the values of a time gone by where quality, freshness and fair prices bag the customers. Common sense and a public desire for fair trade and organic chemical-free food are bringing us back to down-to-Earth values.

The glittery packaging and hard sell of big business no longer holds the attention of those who see through the illusion. Unfortunately there are still a hard core of people who are caught up in the oil boom mentality where they think that Peak Oil and Climate Change predictions are fantasy. The perceived magic of fast foods and convenience products have led us to a place where many have lost the skills of cooking or even understanding where their food comes from. They believe that they can continue to rape and pillage Mother Earth *ad infinitum* and that her resources will never deplete. They see it as their right to take for themselves, selfishly ignoring the health and welfare of the planet or any other creatures that inhabit the surface. People can be fickle and let their loyalties switch to the latest craze at the drop of a hat.

The power of the media which infiltrates most households on a daily basis in the form of TV, newspapers, magazines, radio and internet brings us information to a degree previously unknown. Not all of it is enhancing or beneficial as we are drawn into the personal lives and trivia about celebrities that we do not need to know. Exploitation by using music or film-stars to promote political points of view is commonplace now and we are left with difficulty in knowing who to trust and what to believe. The solidity and connection to our ancestors, our place of birth, our food sources and our ability to communicate with honesty have been driven out of us, replaced instead by a need to emulate the false ideals represented in soap operas.

The majority of the human race has opted for the convenience of electricity, computers and faster transport, seducing us away from the natural slow rhythms of the Earth Mother. Faster lifestyles have led us away from 'Old Magic'. That old power is now held by the trees, the stones, the animals and creatures of nature, and the few people who wear the true cloaks of magic. You may think my comments are more a view on the politics of our current times and not a discussion on magic - but the wise-women of old, the shamanka and priestesses have always used magic to heal the sick, release the dying, feed the many, protect the land and to hold the spirit of the people. They try to do so still - in all parts of the world.

The Environment

The world, our Earth Mother, has matured and changed over millennia and her complex systems have balanced out to maintain a climate in which we can survive. Our tribal ancestors began to settle and farm which started the impact that man has had in contributing to Earth changes. Clearing forests to farm took away much of the carbon dioxide sink and left the soil vulnerable to erosion. All these man-made changes were at a slow enough pace and the Earth's power of recovery was such that the effect on the planet was small. Man's ability to adapt meant that with greater food sources, better shelter and increasing skills the population grew which in turn meant need for larger settlements. Human utilisation of coal, gas and oil sparked industrialisation and catapulted us into a new way of living - and more population rise.

Over the last hundred years the balance and fine-tuning of the world's systems has been under threat as humans have been pumping carbon dioxide into the atmosphere and artificially adding an extra factor into the natural balance equation. Now we have reached a place where the Earth is warming up more quickly than she has done over the last ten thousand years and the changes ahead for the planet and her occupants will be massive. Mother Earth has survived major changes in her history and she no doubt will again.

But our ability to survive with her is now down to our ability to change our way of living.

As we enter the Age of Aquarius and leave the Piscean Age behind, so we leave behind the age of patriarchal power and move into a matriarchal female time. We hear regularly on news reports that the world is in trouble and so perhaps nurturing with some mother energy is what she needs. It could all be quite depressing were it not for the rise in the number of groups promoting community-based environmental projects.

One of these inspirations is the Permaculture Association inspired by the work of Bill Mollison who set out a structure of living and growing based on sound common-sense and old-fashioned need. It promotes organic growing and living symbiotically with the land to make maximum sustainable use of what you have, whether it's a window-box or a farm. Composting and recycling are high on the agenda as well as reading the land to gauge which areas are cold and windy, frost pockets or arid areas with poorer soil. These are things that would have been described to me by Uncle Math as slowing down and taking time to observe the land and how nature wants it to be.

By living in harmony with the Earth again and showing respect for our food and water sources we would become more in tune with the rhythms of the land. If each of us cared for our own immediate neighbourhood the feeling of care and love would begin to grow and the joy in receiving the Earth's abundance would permeate our daily lives. We would come to know the people in our neighbourhood again and we would recreate the extended families we have lost. Enough individuals living this way would create the mass change of mood required for governments to take notice, because only when it's a sure thing on voting merit will they follow public opinion.

The art of changing consciousness at will is magic. Each of us can make our own magic and create change in our own lives, which adds to the bigger picture. The sum of the parts is greater than the whole. We are each connected to the other and to all of life, and to our living Earth - and life is sacred. That which is sacred cannot have a price put on it.

The Transition Town movement is a model of how these changes can be implemented. Built on a design by Rob Hopkins, it examines how sustainable individual communities are in the face of the forthcoming changes of Peak Oil and Climate Change. It encourages people to live again as communities rather than as commuting-type families and to use local shops and facilities. Growing food at home is encouraged and helps to reconnect us to our food sources and to become aware of the distance many forms of food cover before they hit our supermarket shelves. Many pessimists who indulge in the doom and gloom feelings about our future fear that it is too late to do anything against the threats of Peak Oil. One of the beautiful characteristics of the Transition Town movement is the 'do it anyway' theme because the doom and gloom may never happen and these changes can only be better for us and our world. Should the main utility companies fail to provide for us, as has been predicted could happen, causing power cuts, failure of water supplies and gas cuts, then as individuals and as communities we need to care for ourselves and the vulnerable - i.e. sick, young, elderly and disabled. Can we as a community cope and continue to thrive?

I smiled to listen to one of my patients bemoaning life at home where his elderly dad had just moved in with him. Initial welcomings had worn off and the grating between generations were beginning to show as his seventeen year-old son was growing less tolerant of, and less respectful to, his grandfather. My patient listened with frustration to an argument over the TV between grandson and grandfather...

"Oh grandad, you're really stupid - you can't even set a video."

"Aye lad, but you can't set a plough - and where do you think your food comes from?"

Many people do have a conscience and do live with high morals and ethics. We see groups like Friends of the Earth, Greenpeace, Amnesty International, etc. who work to resolve world issues and are driven by the many people who want a fairer, better way of living and a happier world to live in. A group called Parallel Community hopes to link many like-minded souls to encourage a mass voice to speak out against injustices done in the public name. Let's hope that mass consciousness tips the balance of protecting our wild places for themselves and not just for human use.

Those of us who do live consciously (by that I mean aware of every thought and action we make and its impact on those around us and the environment) see the world as a living entity - our Mother who nurtures and nourishes us, and in the bigger picture we humans are only one small element. The spirits of nature are now confined to childrens' stories or seen as fantastical beings like the walking trees in 'Lord of the Rings'. Writings in many of the classic novels are the wisdoms of old committed to stories, but sadly we in our modern world often fail to understand the lesson being conveyed.

I wonder if the landmarks of stone circles were the way the ancients left reminders for us, showing that a previous era held skills and understandings and lessons that should not be lost. Our lands in this country are covered in ancient reminders of the Earth's power spots and these bloody great stones can't fail to draw the attention of the most disconnected human being that the earth beneath them is more energetic and magical than normal. Many of the fairy stories of Scotland, England, Wales and Ireland are connected to these powerful places.

Just being in these environments can raise your own energy enough to allow you to expand your normal levels of tuning in and take you to higher levels of understanding and vision. Remaining open-minded will enable you to hear the messages from the land or the trees by way of an intuited voice or picture in your head, or even by an actual encounter with a magical being. Leylines or fairy roads describe the electromagnetic veins that cover our Earth and the well-trodden old roads and tracks which have gathered the energy of those who have walked them for years. Our ancestors understood how to tune in to the land and be part of that energy enabling their own bodies to feel lighter and raised to a higher vibration. They also understood the unseen entities and beings who form part of our world and respected them rather than feared them as our more recent relatives have done.

The animistic spirituality of Neolithic peoples saw the soul in every rock, tree, plant and animal and gave it due respect and sense of being. Never did they abuse anything they used. The unseen worlds were written about in all the ancient scriptures of all religions. They were written in the Bible and are preached about in this country today in the form of the Angelic Realms and are accepted but little understood.

As well as the obvious places like stone circles, energy in the land can be easily located around where you live. Many of our modern churches are built on top of ancient pagan sites of worship, chosen for the enhanced energy and alignment of the area. Books like Hamish Miller's 'The Sun and the Serpent' describe how a lot of the older churches are built so their east-west alignment coincides with an underlying leyline. You don't have to travel too far from home to find a spot where you can allow yourself to step into a different energy - another world - and tune into the energy of Mother Nature.

Bad Medicine?

I wish I had a pound for every person that came to me saying 'Do you know anything that will cure...?' or 'I don't want to take the drugs the GP gave me any more, do you know anything natural?'. More and more people are beginning to question the drugs pushed at them by both GPs and vets. They are no longer duped into tugging their forelocks to the voice of authority. I guess it's one thing that the internet has done for us - it has made information more readily available and people can research their own conditions and the side-effects of conventional medicine.

But it is becoming clearer that Big Pharma is getting anxious at the knowledge and informed decision-making that takes place by individuals and is coming up with more obscure treatments for diseases and vaccinations for conditions rarely contracted. It is also pressurising restrictions on the sales of vitamins, supplements and herbal remedies available for people to use for self-medication. Could a time come when individuals are refused NHS treatment if they are not vaccinated or taking the prescribed chemicals that earns Big Pharma enough to keep their top executives living in lucrative lifestyles?

We hear criticism for homeopathic remedies because they cannot be proven scientifically. Perhaps we should be criticising medical science for not having the sophistication to prove homeopathy works. This success has been demonstrated for thousands of years. As an ancient form of medicine I think it should be referred to as an 'original medicine' rather than alternative medicine. As a form of treatment that I use regularly with animals, who incidentally have no preconceived idea that they are being given a remedy, I see wonderful changes within a very short space of time and sometimes complete cures on cases deemed 'no-hopers' by conventional forms of medicine.

Some would argue that there is a placebo effect, but this cannot be the case with an animal who doesn't know it has been given a medicine. Others would claim that the intention of the owner has directly affected the change. If this is true, then my feeling is to shout "Hoorah!" that an improvement has taken place and "Hoorah!" that science recognised the power of intent. Intent is the core of true healing and in my opinion whatever the medium it is delivered in is irrelevant if the outcome is successful.

ട൦ത

It is sad that so many people have given the responsibility of their health to their doctor or hospital. Important decisions on their healthcare are often dictated by trends, or needs to meet quotas and targets, rather than the patients health and wellbeing.

Costs of veterinary care have gone through the roof with many practices charging a 75% mark-up on drug costs. This is causing some people to avoid registering their pets and could ultimately be responsible for creating welfare issues. This makes me think we are going backward instead of becoming more enlightened and reminds me of an old farmer who's horse I was treating thirty years ago. When I asked who his vet was he said "Old Harry" who happened to be the local knackerman, "If I can't fix it, Old Harry always will." Current price implications are taking us back to a place where animals may be destroyed rather than treated by vets.

It took me until I was in my forties to be able to talk openly, lecture and even teach healing. Previously I would dismiss what I was doing in an off-hand pseudo-scientific manner as "balancing the energy" or laugh it off saying "My husband just calls me a bloody old Scottish witch". So when I was asked to lecture on healing at a veterinary conference I declined. After being asked for three years in a row, I eventually said yes, wondering where this confident positive reply had come from.

I prepared my presentation only to be told late in the day that I would have to use PowerPoint slides. This was an alien thing to me and as a technophobe still is - to everyone else PowerPoint was a new-fangled piece of technology that those who understand and work with such things were just getting to grips with. My husband came to the rescue and helped change slides into computer-speak. Then they asked if I would do a live demonstration! Well the Universe must have had a hand in what happened that day because I agreed without hesitation and amazingly all went to plan.

One hundred and fifty vets who would normally be quite sceptical about an unscientific intangible treatment listened quietly to my presentation for forty-five minutes. I invited them to step outside to the foyer of the conference centre where the organisers had brought a horse to receive the healing. In my absence, the vets were given the history of the horse and had the opportunity to watch her move and make their diagnosis of her injury. I was only told that she was a mare called Biddy and she was standing just outside.

Without touching, her I analysed her energy by allowing my hands to travel through her aura about three inches above her body. While explaining what I was finding to the watching vets, I was able to predict that "She is relaxing now and will drop her head" - down it went - "I am coming to an area where the energy is distorted, this is an area of pain and she will throw her head up" - up it went - "I am now going to clear the distortion from this place, remove the negative energy and therefore relieve her discomfort, and she should relax again" and her head dropped, bottom lip went gloopy and her eyelids began to get heavy. Biddy was a push-button model, my saviour and accepted the hands-off healing treatment readily.

We went back inside after the demonstration where I said I would try to answer any questions about what they had just witnessed. Fully expecting a barrage of criticism, or at least scepticism, I stood on stage and looked over the forest of hands, and yes there he was - the resident heckler! - a vet who was always very vocal in such situations. I decided to grit my teeth and take his question first to get it out of the way. You can imagine how shocked I was when moist-eyed he said in a trembling voice "That was amazing, for years I have known I could pick up something more with my hands, how can I learn more about this stuff?".

Thanked by the presenter for making it a memorable conference and "One of the most poignant things he'd ever seen", I left the auditorium in a haze of surprise only to be accosted all evening during the dinner dance about what healing could do. As the evening rolled into the wee small hours I was told several times that what I had done earlier had reassured the vets present that healing had a place in their future and that somehow I had united all present in a reality that held some strange meaning for everyone. The horse, by the way, walked away sound at the end of the healing. She had suffered an injury to her off-hind leg the previous week. After the healing, her lack of lameness had convinced even the resident heckler that something positive had happened.

At the end of the evening, a kiss on the cheek by an old Irish greyhound vet was followed by a complimentary comment about Celtic witches and then "Can you put your hands on this bloody bottle now and improve this crap table wine!".

ഔ⊙ൽ

Interestingly, many of the treatments from long ago are classed as whacky modern alternatives and are often brushed off as trivial non-scientific rubbish because they are hard to prove scientifically. Equally the subject of dowsing is dismissed and relegated to the 'weird amusement category' by most media sources. It is interesting to know, however, that most of the big oil, electricity, mining and water companies throughout the world have dowsers on their payrolls hired under the description of researchers or technicians!

As we progress through a future with oil sources gradually depleting we may need to refer back to many of the skills and resources of a time gone by. Unless new inventions of energy to power things and different ways of manufacturing drugs are found, we may have to depend on previously employed methods.

The cloak of illusion that modern methods are better is perpetuated by companies who make big profits. They maintain this myth that nature must be dominated and that anything natural is outdated and bad for you. By slowing down and tuning in to the natural world, we remember that we are part of it. Separation from our living world reduces our ability to tune into the land's sources of energy available to us all.

The best way to reconnect is to spend time in the wild, preferably in remote places, where we can immerse ourselves in our surroundings and soak up the energy of the land. By observing the animals, birds and plants around us, we can learn the secrets of their worlds that will help to put our own into perspective. We will begin to understand that the things that really matter in life have very little to do with fast cars, new hi-fi's, computers or mobile phones. Our homes should be a place of safety, providing warmth and protection - but when our homes involve us in working to pay huge mortgages and hire purchase payments for expensive furnishings they become a source of stress and worry instead.

Let's start peering behind the cloak of illusion and find the strength to stand in our own space and make our own choices and decisions about how we want to live - from medical, religious, political, economic choices to affordable, sustainable living. Only we can change our world. Magic can help us do this, and magic may be essential to do this, but it will not do it for us, it will only support us in doing it.

Words have Power

The Bible tells us 'In the beginning there was the Word' and in this busy life we all lead, one of our problems is that we do not choose our words very carefully. Bad examples are witnessed regularly, we only need to switch on the telly to hear swearing and cursing - literally cursing - on our many well-watched soap operas. Words have power!

Listen for the Truth

Well chosen words have the power to heal as well as harm, as I was taught by the old ones. The old wise-women and shamen across the world were recognised for their ability to articulate their wisdom. Knowing when to speak and when to listen was taught in the mystery schools when teaching was passed on verbally rather than by the written word.

In many of the old drawings depicting the Greek god Hermes, we see him holding his forefinger to his lips as though in a 'sshh' gesture. These drawings showed gestures used in the Hermetic mystery schools when students were required to be quiet and concentrate. This was the indication to neophytes in training that this was an important thing to listen to as it was a wisdom being passed down and had to be logged in their memories. The reason given by all priests and priestesses through time right up to today is that this wisdom is only for trainees of the mysteries, as important information misused in the wrong hands has the ability to be harmful. Over time, as we have discussed, this has caused a division and meant that the ill-informed common man has not taken responsibility for his own spiritual connection as he has been lead to believe that his God would not hear his word unless it was passed on by priests who had His ear.

Much of the lore was passed down through generations with each adding to the long list to be committed to memory. Sometimes this was made easier by including the wisdom to be memorised within a song or a story. The danger of this has been that although many sagas and stories have survived, their true meanings have been lost and many of the words have been changed over time like Chinese whispers, completely altering their meaning.

In Scotland the influx of religious passion in the shape of Catholicism crept across the country in the early years and was preached to the people by educated men, with an air of authority. The country communities of farming people would naturally bow down to the superiority of this educated voice and the traditional laws of hospitality would accept them into their communities.

Several things happened simultaneously around this time. First the local people were talking Gaelic and services preached to them in English, let alone Latin, were not understood. As a result many people had dual faiths, where they quietly and secretly continued to revere nature and the land, celebrating the cycles of seasons with their festivals on the quarter and cross-quarter days and yet would attend the church because it was the 'right' thing to do to stay in favour with the authorities. Secondly the wave of Protestantism to counter the Catholic church set the political battles in place that continue to this day. To the ignorant farm workers and country dwellers this level of theologistic debate was beyond them and they would be most likely to keep favour with whichever side was most beneficial to their lifestyle whilst quietly following their own belief system.

With the more educated priests and scholars came the ability to write and record much of the lore previously only spoken. Sadly much of what was committed to the written form was these academic scholars' interpretations of what they heard. As a result, much of the history - for example that of the faerie-folk - has been reduced to stories to entertain or chide children, seeming too far-fetched to be considered anything but fancy to such learned gentlemen. Still the debate on the theories of faeries raged on right up into the 1900's where opinions of a foreign race, spirits or ghosts or pure imagination were put forward in the shape of scientific research of folklore and belief.

Certainly the feeling of placing such wonders in the realms of fantasy became common practice by those who wished to appear educated or gentry, and has let me understand my mother's need to dismiss my childhood observations fearfully as lies.

I remember being told by an elder "Be careful what you ask for as your wish may be granted" and saw that illustrated when a work colleague went off for a long-sought-after holiday. For weeks she had said she was desperate for a break and looked forward to her three-week-long trip. She returned after one week, having slipped and broken her wrist - not quite the break she desired - but of course she had not been specific in her wish.

Being clear and specific in your choice of words is obviously important in our daily lives - even more important in affirmations we make or spells we cast. When we say 'I want more money' the message we send out to the aether is 'I want' and so we will continue to want more money. Instead we should visualise having that money and affirm 'I have lots of money' - if of course that is what we desire. Choose your words carefully in all walks of life as many words cast in anger are said without thought and regretted later. Take a moment to think it through, as you should never have to live with the feeling that you wish you could take your words back. Anything said should be said with honesty and intention from the heart. Everything from 'I love you' all the way through to 'I hate you'. They do have an effect on the recipient, so never use them carelessly.

Old languages like Gaelic and Sanskrit use inbuilt structures to observe courtesies of age or authority by phrasing things differently. There is no material possession in the old Gaelic language and so one would not say 'This is my coat' - it would be 'This is the coat I am wearing'. 'This is my dog' would be said as 'This is the dog that is with me'. I find this intriguing and wonderful when we have moved so far away from this to a world where so much is gauged by material possessions. There is strength in these gentle old languages where the lilts and tones soothe the soul and phrases were carefully considered.

෨⊙ඣ

Some years ago I came across a flyer for a conference being held in London. It was for a talk by Professor Masaru Emoto and his fascinating work on water. I had heard of his work and was interested by an approach that was scientific but open to the spiritual. Perhaps he would be able to represent things in a way I was unable to. Always keen to further my knowledge and be wowed by someone else's magic I bought tickets for my husband Dave and myself. After organising our children we travelled to London for an exciting evening full of expectation, when I would be able to hear from the man himself how he had gone about this enlightening study.

A packed full house of mainly academics gathered in the auditorium in a prestigious building and we all stared at the screen on-stage with the projected image of an enlarged frozen water crystal and a heading in English reading Messages from Water. A dapper, suited Japanese gentleman came on-stage accompanied by a Japanese woman with long black hair and wearing a smart red jacket, who announced that she was going to be Mr Emoto's interpreter. The audience's disappointment was compounded when the Professor's long enthusiastic Japanese ramble was interpreted as a short abrupt sentence of jumbled pigeon English. Rumblings began in the crowd, several people got up and left and then a couple of brave souls raised their hands and asked for a fuller description of what Mr Emoto was so clearly animated about.

What happened next left me dumb-founded and to this day I cannot comprehend if it was some deep message or a grossly stupid mistake on somebody's part, but Mr Emoto himself then addressed the audience in perfect English and began to expound in long, clear descriptive explanations about the work he was presenting. This strange beginning somehow distracted from the wondrous pictures and meanings of his theories. We were left at the end somewhat jarred by the energy of the meeting, but I did buy his books and took great pleasure in digesting them later.

The books described how he had started studying water after meeting with a Californian scientist. Using advanced technology he went on to look at the effect that water had on humans and the effect that humans had on water. By studying the crystals of water that had been frozen and put under a strong microscope he could compare the shape of a beautiful crystal from a clear mountain springs with the distorted broken crystal shapes of polluted city rivers. Developing this study further he looked at water exposed to various plants and found that the crystals always developed the same shapes - a beginning of the explanation of homeopathy perhaps - and then he examined water exposed to various types of music and again found some consistencies and comparisons.

Further extension of this theory led him to expose water to words of love and words of hate, and astonishing pictures of the frozen crystals were produced. The water given words of love and appreciation produced delicate star-shaped crystals similar to the archetypal picture of a snowflake. The water exposed to words of hate and anger hardly looked like crystals at all - they were unformed, misshapen splodges.

Given that the amount of water in our bodies is about 70% and the surface of the planet about 70%, we can see the effect our words can have not only on another human being but on Mother Earth herself.

Like many others trying to present a new approach, Masaru Emoto's work has been knocked and mocked, and certainly he did not endear himself to the majority of the conference members when I attended. But this man's work is thoughtful and energetic and is criticised by a body of scientists who have a closed mind to the quantum side of physics. Similar to the put-downs of homeopathy, acupuncture and chiropractic work, this work has not been studied and evaluated in an open-minded and fair way.

Those of us prepared to look beyond a faltering presentation, a cultural difference, a less-than perfect scientific research and just be open to the suggestion of Professor Emoto's work, can see the value to humankind and science of this study. If we can take seriously that our words can have a profound effect on those we direct them to, then we must carefully consider what we think and say and listen to.

Consider if you will that we can raise the health and well-being of an individual, a community, a country and eventually a planet, by the words we choose. Using a conscious choice of words to respond and a tone of voice gentle in its delivery can raise an individual's energy and make them feel good. Can you imagine a whole community doing this for one another - how good would it be to live in that energy? That would be true magic. Equally we witness the opposite in our society - but it is ultimately our choice as to how we respond. If each of us paid heed to our own life the overall change could occur when the mass consciousness is large enough to tip the balance in favour of love and well-being.

Mentors, Paths and Truths

If you are lucky, you will find a mentor who can guide you. Guiding is quite different from teaching and it is important that the mentor you find allows you to walk your own path and doesn't insist that you follow theirs. To find a person like this is a real gift as so many people allow their own egos to get in the way of supporting another.

I have been very lucky to have found several people along my journey who have encouraged me but kept their own and my egos at bay. From the old men present during my childhood to my dear friend and mentor Sue, I have been guided by good, down-to-earth advice - which is not always easy to take! We all know that the truth can hurt, but sometimes only a true friend with your interests at heart can care enough to risk hurting you with the truth.

I asked Sue why she did not use a 'given name' like so many adepts seem to do. She immediately turned it round and asked why I didn't use one. I explained that I was offered one once while in a deep trance journey from an ancient master, but that I had politely declined the offer.

"Why did you turn it down?" she challenged me.

"Because I am on my own path and I am just me being me!"

"Exactly - that's the whole fucking point" she chided.

I'm sure that many of the "Blossoming Moon Flowers" and "Sai Bahtvas" have genuinely been given the names they assume and follow the path of their beliefs, but I also believe that some adopt it like an actor's stage name and pretend their journey.

I have just spent a weekend with a group of energetically aware women in a roundhouse in Dartmoor. We were exploring our journeys into shadow - the dark night of the soul. Strong powerful women, nine of us altogether, held the space as we each journeyed to the bottom of the cauldron and dissolved our pain and suffering. The 'cauldron' is a symbolic term describing the vessels that our ancient ancestors believed held the energy centres and soul in the body. This gathering allowed us to work on past hurts still held energetically in the psyche, creating blocks to our development. Transforming pain into the path of healing is a major part of magic. Yet I was surprised to hear, even from these experienced women, a level of disappointment in their own abilities in magic. I found it hard to understand how some of them worked at this level and yet had missed the fundamental point of what magic is. What were they expecting? What were their experiences?

In deep discussion with a couple of them I questioned their disappointment and pointed out their achievements. "Oh yes, I understand all that but I suppose I want to see immediate changes like Harry Potter's 'Reparo charm' or 'Wingardium Leviosa' so I can really believe it's real!" one of my friends told me. Perhaps this level of insecurity and disbelief stems from a lack of backup and support, because we no longer live nurtured by that sort of culture.

My experiences of words of power have been both on the giving and receiving ends. Words aimed at me with power and venom have stayed with me forever and I have had to work so very hard to release myself from their hold. Tones of voice have implied loathing and cut me to the bone, and yet I also remember the implied love and caring when words were given in a compassionate gentle tone and soothed my soul at the time they were offered.

If we think back to our childhoods and how we were spoken to then, it can give us clues as to how we respond to words now. If you were constantly shouted at, then the words spoken were less relevant than the tone of voice and can be a trigger in adulthood. The familiarity of that noise may also lead you to shout at your own children, perpetuating the nastiness of this type of communication. How often do we respond out of habit rather than from conscious thought?

My Dad's phrase which has stuck in my mind comes back to me now in this discussion - he said "With Truth as your sword you will win all battles". I saw this illustrated clearly in 2007 when I was a victim of an identity theft. My blunt honesty exposed the man who had used my name, identity and circumstances to fraudulently accrue a large amount of money. Although nothing was physically taken from me, my character and reputation could have been damaged and my ability to borrow money completely ruined. In business terms it could have been a disaster.

However, the man was arrested and I had to give a long witness statement to the Police and was called to Court as chief witness.

Even as an innocent victim, High Court is a very intimidating place and makes one feel nervous. I had been guided by the Police that the prosecution barrister would lead me through my statement to set the scene, but to be prepared that this man's barrister, the defence counsel, would try to discredit my statement and so to expect a very long and arduous grilling.

I sat in the Witness Box shaking but slightly cross that this thief was lounging in the dock with an air of smugness. The prosecuting barrister started to question me and I stuttered nervously as I scrabbled for my specs and fumbled to find the correct page of the statement. After a good fifteen minutes, I was passed on to the defence counsel. I cringed to think how badly I had answered already - and that was the easy bit - now the difficult bit was about to start.

I'm sure I would have discredited myself in some way and allowed this man to squirm out of his capture had it not been for his barrister who strutted in front of me. His attitude of confident superiority, added to his client's smugness, was at odds with what I understood as the truth - right from wrong. Then without looking at me, and addressing the Judge and jury, he began his argument...

"Dr Simon, may I suggest that what you actually heard was ...!" and "May I suggest that what my client actually said was...!" The red mist came down, truth WAS my sword and without stutter, judder or nervousness I threw down my statement, removed my spectacles and in a loud, clear authoritative voice directed straight at my questioner, I said:

"No, you may not suggest this, as it would be a complete lie!" The jury gasped, the Judge stopped writing and peered at me - then at the barrister - over his glasses. The man in the dock sat bolt upright and grabbed at the edge of the box while my inquisitor gaped like a goldfish and shuffled his papers.

"No more questions, My Lord", he eventually said. I was directed out of the box by the Clerk of the Court, surprised that my long grilling was over so quickly. The

Policewoman who had worked on the case was surprised - "How did you do that?" she squeaked.

"I just told the truth" I answered. The thief was given two years and I was not called again. That ring of truth has power - my Dad was right.

ഇ⊙ൽ

The sun grows warmer and the bell from the abbey down the valley 'dongs' the nuns to Office. The early Sunday stillness holds the world at bay and Nature breathes in, letting me feel the pulse of the land, just stirring gently at the early part of the year. I am surrounded by birds beginning to pair, my hens, my dogs and a bee laden with yellow pollen from the hazel catkins in her little leg-baskets, my family still snoozing in bed, but I am aware of being alone. The metallic bell catches my attention and draws my thoughts to the ordered but secluded lives the nuns live within their closed Order. Then I drift to another time...

The Glas-Ghairm

2276 years ago…

Tucked into the hillside almost unseen against the barren surroundings was a dwelling. It was made from granite boulders and covered in turf, rendering it largely invisible but for a wisp of smoke escaping through the grassy roof and some plants, logs and animal bones outside it. Several yards behind and to the right as you face it lay an ancient forest of thick Caledonian pine and to its left lay the rest of the bare promontory bravely pushing into a wild grey sea below. It was cold in the north of Scotland, the rugged and rocky west coast being exposed to the Atlantic storms of winter. But within the boundary of this dwelling there was a peace and a sense of love and calm that permeated anything that came within it.

In the dwelling lived a woman called Meg. Some called her Mary, but that was her title and not her name, and in the Gaelic language she was known as Mhairi. Meg lived alone; that is without another human with her. The people from the nearby clans occasionally visited asking for help with some problem, a cure for an illness or a blessing of some sort. Others feared her and stayed away. These were usually the ones who had something to hide or to be ashamed of and they knew her power of sight would find their secret. Her power of sight did - it was able to have a grasp of everything and everyone in the local communities, the relationships both legitimate and covert, and the animals, the weather, and the crops.

The only other creatures who shared her home were animals who were sick or those who came to spend time with this solitary soul of their own volition. Some were previous patients and others were passing friends or old-time friends. They were greeted with reverence and given food and bedding and a welcome to the fire like any other guest. What was strange was that these animals were often large predators like wolves, bears or eagles, but in Meg's home they were as gentle as some of the deer calves, cats or lambs that they often shared the space with.

Meg was a crone whose skills at healing and seeing had come down through her family. Known as a curser, her skills were used to drive out sickness or illness, to reduce tumours or to send away blights of the crops. Her abilities were known of far and wide and it was not unusual for grand visitors from other tribes and clans, or even other countries, to visit asking for her services. For this they paid her well but often in gold or jewels that held no value for Meg. These things she traded on for flour or cloth or herbs from foreign lands, which let her live a healthy life and she could continue to astound her regular clientele with new knowledge and healing potions.

The trade routes through Iona and Mull several days south of her were busy and the traders came for the rich deposits of gold and silver. Boats did come in further up the west coast but the steep rocky shorelines were dangerous in anything but calm weather, especially for the bigger boats. So most travelled cross county from what we now call Oban.

Regularly Meg would skry to view beyond her boundaries and was not surprised to see a ship come into Iona carrying two men and a boy who had travelled from the exotic lands to the east. She knew they were special and that they were going to visit her. But she was also aware of something else that carried a sense of foreboding. The older of the two men was a man she knew of and was a powerful man - one she would have described as sidhe or 'shining one'. She was humble and respectful of his power - not a thing common to this woman. She laughed in her vision to see this man bare-footed and bare-legged in the bitter cold of the early part of the Scottish year. So she set to make him trews and leggings like the local tribesmen wore beneath the plaid, and a lambskin top that he could wear beneath his wrap. Her skills of craftwork were exceptional and she finished the garments in good time to apply the adornments of grandeur fitting for her visitor and gifts for those accompanying him. The day before they arrived she set to cleaning and tidying her home and asking her animal guests to move outside. She made bread and prepared soup for her guests. The local people became aware that Meg was preparing for guests but no word had come by conventional routes that anyone was on their way.

At the end of her cleaning and preparing she went down to the sea. It was not unusual to see her do this as she frequently went to commune with the seals, dolphins and whales that inhabited the waters and visited her bay at the foot of the promontory. But today she was carrying her best clothes and ritual cloak because she was preparing a cleansing ritual. Unwrapping herself from her dirty ragged layers of clothing she plunged under the surface of the icy brine as she uttered the words of a spell for cleansing. Dressed and back in her home, she combed the endless tugs from her hair, washed her raggy cloths, then adorned herself in her amulets of power as she waited for her guests.

Early next morning a young boy from a nearby clan ran in calling warning to Meg that the men were coming. Paid with the gift of eggs for his mother he left slowly, wanting to witness the meeting. Meg busied herself, sorting the skins for them to sit on, organised last bits of the meal she was preparing, tidied her hair and put water on to boil. She looked out the gifts of leggings, hats and tunics she had made for them, and then waited at the crest of the hill for them. In the distance she could see two men and a boy approach leading horses packed with supplies. To her it was strange to see men walk rather than ride as she reckoned local men would ride rather than walk to the midden.

Meg recognised the old man walking, leaning heavily on his staff, as the man from her vision. He carried an air of authority like the merlins or powerful shamen from these lands, so her stomach lurched a little, but she held her space and power, awaiting his greeting. Heavily accented, he addressed her in her native tongue and dropped onto one knee in a gesture of respect, asking for her hospitality. She walked forward offering her hand in greeting and inviting this man who called himself Joseph into her humble home.

They ate and talked politely of trivial things. She asked about his journey and of the local area he had just travelled through. A discussion of the food, which included honey she had gathered in the forest allowed her to describe her surroundings and confirmed her skills in country lore that had encouraged him to find her. All the time she was gathering information about the surrounding lands he had crossed. But she was also realising that he had a hesitance to come to the point, which meant that his purpose was serious. This was as she had gleaned from her vision, but the details still evaded her. Then she asked of his country and his expression changed to a serious one. Shooing his companion and the boy from the house, Joseph and Meg started discussions that went on until late in the afternoon. Joseph described the situation in his homelands, he told of oppression and slavery by a cruel ruler. Then he made his request of her. He asked that she place a curse on the guards so that his people could escape.

The enormity and depth of challenge of this task made her gasp. Meg's mind raced feeling fear, pride of being asked, wonder about how she could accomplish so big a undertaking through to emptiness in the pit of her stomach as she realised that this was a request that she knew in her heart was hers to do, but that to do it would cause her death.

She had to consider carefully as the implications were far-reaching. If it worked, it could change the course of history and that she questioned - would she want to be responsible for this? If it worked...! She knew she could do it. Torn between the challenge to her skills and the effects of its success and the consequences to her she walked outside leaving her guest by the fire.

The fresh wind that blew in off the sea had died and the air was still and expectant. The wren - king of birds - that had befriended her, jigged in and out of her woodpile, his small black eye watching her troubled concentration. Meg headed to the trees first and was aware of the grey wolf loping quietly behind and to her left - a cub she had reared some years before, found abandoned under a tree-stump. The sky pinked and a light veil of snow dropped between the trees turning the frosty floor white. Silence and stillness fell around her as if the woods were holding their breath and awaiting her decision. The wild ones came out from their homes to watch as Meg passed. She did so in silence, lost in thought, and they worried for her as she would normally have acknowledged their presence. As quickly as it had started the snow stopped and the sun brightened the watery sky, the trees dropped their silver jewels onto the white carpet and Meg walked back towards to sea shore - she would consult the elders who swam in the ocean, Mother Earth's great womb.

Still dressed in her best robes she walked into the sea to her knees, the ice-cold water sharpening her senses, and she called out to the whales. These great old mothers were headed north to the feeding grounds near the ice and she asked for audience with them. Meg's powers as a caller proved strong as a great blow of spray spumed near the end of the promontory. Lifting her skirts she hurried with numb bare feet along the slippery rocks to greet this great whale and she poured out her story and her fears. A seeing eye broke the surface and looked into Meg's soul - she had her answer.

Content in her heart that this was her task she walked quickly back to her home - her fate was sealed but she would worry about that later. Now she had a job to do and she had decided that if she had to do it then her task was to achieve it without harming a soul. She would not hold that in her conscience. As she entered the dwelling, her ruddy face radiant, Joseph smiled - he had his answer too, now it was time to plan the details. For the next two days Meg and Joseph were steeped in planning, his companion and the boy gathered wood for the fire and prepared the food that Meg had left out. Then it was time for the visitors to leave.

From the pack bundles, Joseph brought out gifts for Meg, benzoain gum, myrrh, fine linen cloths and jugs of fine wine from his lands. Then from a blue cloth he unwrapped a sphere of lapis lazuli streaked with gold with a hole drilled through where a strange-shaped leather thong was attached. He hung it round her neck and hugged her close. No words could express the feelings that flowed between them - respect, gratitude, understanding, sadness, desperation, anxiety, joy and excitement - all wrapped up in a close hug. Meg helped them pack and gave them food for the journey - home-made cheese, dried fruit and cold meat, and then watched as they moved off, Joseph in his warm clothing, his feet caressed in skin shoes. Meg settled back into her seat by the fire, mulling over all that had happened over the last few days.

A sense of pride washed over her as she realised how far this man had come to ask for her help but that was quickly diluted by a gnawing fear in her gut of what lay ahead.

Always practical, she busied about checking the moon phases and the forthcoming weather and to plan exactly how she would carry out her task. Determined that she would harm none, her plan was to travel out of body and cast the glas-ghairm - a silencing curse that would hush the animals and stop the dogs barking so the captives could leave the city un-noticed. Adding in a locking charm she could ensure the soldiers, if alerted, could not get out of the building giving her wards a good head start and hopefully preventing any bloodshed. She would do it all at the still of night, on the night of a bright moon to aid their journey.

Many meditations later, checking and rechecking details, astral travelling to examine the site, yet all the while trying to remain cloaked from other skryers' senses, Meg was almost ready to perform her task.

Early one morning on the phase of a full moon, Meg began to arrange her tools and prepare her workspace in her little home. She asked her animal friends to leave, fearing for their safety. She banked up her fire and had spare wood to hand. She laid incense where she could easily reach out her hand to grab it without breaking her trance - a glass of water - her shawl - her crystals of power - her staff - her amulets, the foot of a hawk, wing of a raven, bone of a horse, tooth of a wolf - help from her animal friends without having to call them into a battle that was not theirs. But she knew if she was in trouble she could find them nearby. What else might she need? She could not foresee any other possible situation that had not already been catered for. She wished now for another who could back her power and hold her safe in her journey, a friend who could be depended upon to help her return should she reach disaster. But Meg had no-one - she had always worked as an individual, always alone but for her animals.

All prepared she sat and waited for the moment to come. Too soon and she might attract unwanted attention. The time came round, it was time to act - she dropped onto her horse-skin rug, wrapped her cloak around her and checked the fire, her tools and looked round her home once more - door locked ... ready. Breathing deeply she dropped into a trance state - a glance back at the hunched shape under the shawl, hoping she would return - she sped on the astral planes over the deserts and from above looked down on the great city.

All seemed still - this might be easier than she thought! - until she became aware of the numbers of souls she was to help pass out of the city unseen. Then she realised the scale of the problem - thousands of men, women and children hoping to escape to freedom with her help. She set to work, she had to work fast, she couldn't stay out of her body too long. Her plans were useful but now here in place there were things to fine-tune and some to change.

The silencing curse was of use and so was the locking charm but if she used one curse that would lock the tongues of those alerted, be they man or beast, as well as locking the doors, then she could kill two birds with one stone. She would also have to do two cloaking spells, the first to aid those escaping, the other to prevent her astral body being seen or recognised by the all-seeing eyes of other skryers. She had been told by Joseph that the king of this land had powerful Magi in his pay, and they would be quick to find her and destroy her if they became aware of her presence. Although she was aware of the dangers of this mission and had sensed its bleak outcome, Meg wanted to live and would take every possible precaution to do so.

Positioned over the centre of the city she uttered her curse, describing its boundaries and recipients.

...Toghairmim ubag a chasgadh coin o thaban, no a
glas-ghearm
Na gaireadh na coin no gu n gaireadh na gaimhne
Do gair tri ceo than & ceothan crith & Gaothan-ear
on ailbhina chiuin
Mara ah'ordaich Righ nan Dúl...

...I induce an incantation to prevent the dogs
barking or the lock cry
May the dogs not cry till the cattle call up
I summon three mists and trembling mists
And an east wind from the calm aether as the Lord
of the Elements has ordained...

At that, the dogs and cats and soldiers tongues were
stuck to the roofs of their mouths. The doors were locked
shut, unable to be opened. A wind blew up the dust so that
no-one could see in the inner city but on the outskirts by
the river a cloaking mist appeared. On she called, holding
the space to allow most to pass when suddenly behind her
she saw black black shapes hurtle towards her. Meg
realised she had been seen and could do no more to help -
now she had to return to her body - if she could.

The black shapes got closer, then suddenly turned into
great eagles whose claws raked at her. Meg shape-shifted
into a tiny fly, so small she could not be seen. She moved
away quickly and became her own astral shape again. She
called upon the powers available to her to help her get
home even for a short while. Suddenly, there they were
again - this time they became streaks of lightening
cracking towards her. Meg became the wind and blew
harder creating great clouds of rain and dust over the city
causing enough confusion in which to distract her
pursuers and allow her to shift into her own shape and
return rapidly to her own lands.

In the northwest of Scotland it was dark and cold. Within her howf the candle had burned low, leaving a pool of wax and a barely-lit wick. The fire remains were little red embers within the powdered grey ash. There slumped beneath the cloak lay the empty body of Meg, cold and grey. She was tempted to remain light and free but the drive to return spurred her on to enter her body. With a gasp and a racking cough, she returned to her body now stiff, achy and as cold as stone. She reached for the water and food nearby to help her ground back into herself. Crawling into the hearth she piled kindling onto the embers which broke into flames, and Meg welcomed the light and the warmth. Struggling, she fed the flames and slowly her body thawed and her breathing calmed and she could believe she had made it home.

After a while, Meg walked stiffly to the door and opened it to the familiar star-jewelled sky outside. Not only did she need to see that all was still there but she quietly hoped that a few of her animal friends might come and share her fire as tonight this lone practitioner wanted company. Tomorrow was time enough to reflect on what she had achieved and how she had fared. Tonight, the warmth of a wolf's coarse body and the protection of an all-seeing owl were gifts that made her weep.

Meg sank into sleep on her skins knowing that the Exodus had begun - the Children of Israel were free - and her task was complete.

In the weeks that followed she reflected on what she had done and being the perfectionist she was found places where she could have performed better. Inside she quietly glowed at achieving her mission and returning home to see her animal friends and her home country. But she also had a little nagging feeling that her original sense was true and that her task would cost her her life. So Meg was not surprised when in early summer on her return from the edge of the promontory she was confronted by a soldier clad in leather and clearly from Egypt.

Not sure if he was an apparition or a sending she thought of how she had left her home and what animals were currently in her care. She knew that the local villagers observed her comings and goings with curiosity but kept a respectful distance: they would notice her absence eventually. Knowing that Mairi, a quiet girl from the nearby clan who she had been teaching and who she hoped would one day become a Mary, would move into her home and care for her animals should she be gone, she resolved to accept her fate. In some ways it relieved her of the gnawing anticipation.

Meg wrapped her cloak around her and dropped her defences. A blast of energy swept her off the headland and into the seas below. Dragged under by her clothing, Meg relaxed into the dreamy lullaby of the Earth Mother's womb and in the most peaceful of sleeps, left that life - her body given to the deep.

Using the Skills

I know Meg's story well - it has left me in gasping sobs recalling it and committing it to paper, because Meg was one of my past lifes - the third oldest I can remember. Her skill as a caller came through from a previous life too, from back in the lands of ice 27,000 years ago. This is the fourth and earliest life I have memories of when I was a Neanderthal shaman - a caller.

Flight of the Callers

The caller's role was to locate migrating herds, identify that location and map a route to it from where the clan was based. If very far from the home-base, the caller would try to influence the herd and turn it towards the hunters or to a place where it could be more easily trapped. It was not unusual for them to drive herds over cliffs, which was the easiest way to do a mass killing, though there was less kudos to be gained by the individual hunters.

It was important for these Neanderthal people's to make their kills as close to their winter homes (usually caves) as possible because the carcasses had to be processed quickly and stored for the winter. Every part was used - the skins, bones, fat, meat, internal organs, hair - all had a use and were important to get the clan through the long harsh winter. To transport it was heavy dangerous work as all was carried by the humans who often had to run the gauntlet of other predators who might steal the catch from them. If too far away, then the meat would have to be butchered and dried to preserve it for transportation, but again this would attract other hungry meat-eaters who would quickly detect the smells.

So the callers would try to bring the herd to a closer site. They would do this by travelling in a shamanic trance into the mind of the beasts they were pursuing either mammoth or bison-type beasts or deer/moose-type animals. Then they would merge into the herd instinct, becoming part of it. Their skill was in not losing their mind to the herd but remaining detached enough to remember the master-plan of directing it to the hunters whilst still being in a fleeing animals' senses. It was all too easy to become so immersed in the herd that the caller's instinct was to sympathise and protect the herd, driving it to safety away from the hunters. Clearly, too much empathy would leave the clan hungry that winter and ruin your reputation as a caller. A skilled caller was placed in high regard and would always be given the prime parts of the catch and was cared for by the clan.

My memories of this life are of me, then a male shaman, sitting round a smoky fire within a skin tent. I was throwing incense onto the fire which released oils which helped to induce the magical flight of the shaman. Two others, younger shamen, sat with me to protect me and help to bring me back should I travel too far. I remember the sting of my eyes and the choking smoke as I leaned into the fire and inhaled, drawing the drug into my brain. Suddenly I was flying through blinding snow, the vortex dragging me in faster and faster until there below me ran the herd. White backs, sides streaked with sweat, puffing bellows of breath from rounded muzzles, the eyes glazed in travelling mode - the one mind of the herd. I moved to the leader at the front, his eyes alert, his brain functioning at a different level, he was guiding and directing this thundering mass who pushed him from behind. He was the one who I needed to connect with to turn the herd to the west and slow it down. As I tuned in I felt his fear and he pounded harder and faster - No, I had to dull my thoughts, enter herd mind and lean on his right shoulder. As I changed my thinking this stream of running flesh slowly wheeled to the left heading west towards the valley. I withdrew from the herd and returned to the smoky tent and the chanting of my two colleagues accompanied by the rattling of a deer-toe rattle.

I have had other flashes of this life when I was collecting herbs and lichens from rocks and trees and the thing that is most striking to me, apart from being a man, is the different way of thinking. It felt sluggish and limited in some ways to me, with difficulties in skills like organising and in lateral thought. Yet it was so sharp in instinct and awareness and this shaman was so reverent of, and connected to, the natural world around him. I treat these glimpses as a real gift.

The skills of the callers have passed down through the DNA of these ancestors to many people today. The only callers still practicing in the old way may be the tribal peoples living on the plains-type landscapes in perhaps Africa or Siberia where vast swathes of land are covered to hunt. So many hunting areas have now been reduced because of modern life encroaching that this old skill is hardly required anymore, and many tribes who still hunt for meat do so in the jungle where different skills are employed.

The gift of the caller is mainly found now in people like myself who have a natural affinity with animals. They may work as anything from a dog trainer, a horseman, a vet or even a sheep farmer whose sixth sense will guide him to some lost sheep on a vast mountainside.

This led me to examine how I use this gift in everyday life. My ability to intuit my patient's level of pain and areas of discomfort stems from that skill to tune in to the mind of the herd - but without any herbal aids. Counselling my human patients and 'seeing' their problems and gently offering down-to-earth opinions on their choices comes from the wisdom of the old shamen. I assess the animals' distress and gauge their responses, reading when aggression might appear and diffusing the situation before anyone gets hurt. I offer a physical treatment based on a practical scientific approach but I'm still guided intuitively to work at the required depth. I journey shamanically to feel my patient's pain and travel within their systems to find the underlying causes of their problems. Healing is offered to aid their own support systems and pain drawn out and energy given.

Following the seasonal and moon cycles I travel with nature and glean what Mother Earth offers me. This replenishes my own energies and allows me to offer more to my patients. Always aware of the land I travel through I am in constant contact with the living planet, just as I would have been thousands of years ago. Being in tune lets me examine my feelings for changes and I become aware of many situations before they happen.

ഇ ☉ ങ

In 2000 I was asked to treat a dog who had suffered with epilepsy and had had several fits which his owner worried might have affected his neck. The request came from a patient I knew well and he explained that this dog belonged to a friend of his who happened to be a ventriloquist who lived in London. I immediately thought this was a wind-up and pictured me laying my hands on this dog and a voice saying "Ouch that hurts". It was however genuine and it turned out this owner was also a talented comedian who had been leaving a theatre late one night when a passing truck threw out a bundle in his direction.

Instinctively he caught it. It turned out to be a little mongrel bitch who was about to whelp. She gave birth a short while later to five healthy dog pups which the comedian kept and incorporated them all into a hilarious stage show. The dogs sat, one wearing sunglasses, one a hat, one a scarf and just did their own thing while their owner improvised a comical conversation around their movements. Then, sadly, one little dog had developed a batch of seizures, and my patient had suggested that my treatment might help.

All was arranged, the ventriloquist and his dogs were going to come to my patient's house and I would go there to treat this dog. I arrived and met this lovely man who adored his dogs and did the treatment. He was so pleased with what I had done that when I returned to do the follow-up treatment two weeks later he asked if I would check the other dogs too.

I started with my original patient who hadn't had a fit since I had treated him. Then I started to work through the other dogs. All was going well considering we had three humans and seven dogs, including the house-owner's own dog, squashed into a tiny sitting-room. Ken, the comedian, asked if I could also check the little bitch, mum of the five pups. She was sitting on the settee cuddling into her owner, unlike the boy dogs who were on the floor. So I moved from my place on the floor and sat beside her on the settee. As usual I tuned in to her energy before beginning my examination and the sense of 'Fuck off' from this dog was overwhelming even though she hadn't moved a muscle.

I explained to Ken that she actually didn't want me to touch her but he insisted that given her abuse by her previous owner he would really like me to check her out. So I persevered and against my better judgement I adjusted her neck and through her back. No growls or snarls were uttered but my sense that this dog really wanted me to stop persisted and so, true to my ethics, I explained this and halted the treatment. Ken felt pleased that I had done most of her and accepted my reasoning, feeling happy that I was respecting his dog's sensitivity.

I moved back to where I had been sitting on the floor and began to write my notes up. Then I got a sense of being stared at and looked up to see this bitch with 'Jedi eyes' staring at me. As I watched she looked from me to one of the dogs, a deep meaningful look, then looked back to me. The dog got up and walked towards me where I was still sitting on the floor. I knew in my heart that the communication was 'Get her! That's my boy.' like some matriarchal gangster mother getting her heavies to do the dirty work.

As her boy lumbered towards me I became aware that he was going to bite me, so I started to move to stand up. As this dog was half-way towards me the little epileptic dog hit him broadside with a bark and snarl as if to say 'No, she's my pal.' and suddenly a six-dog fight started as everyone piled in and fur flew. I looked at the bitch, still sat on the settee like the queen mum, who eye-balled me then turned round and curled down on the settee as if settling for sleep as we three humans grabbed scruffs and collars and turfed all the gangsters into the garden, and silence fell in the room.

"What the hell happened?" asked our host.

"Well for fear of babbling anthropomorphic rubbish" I said "I hesitate to say what I really think, but I could swear the little bitch ordered it!" Then Ken said "I think she told her boy to have you - she doesn't like being messed around with". I was relieved it was not just my imagination, someone else had seen it too and to this day I am certain that what I thought I saw was actually real. I have never experienced anything like it before or since, but my sense of understanding of this situation rings true to me.

So I continue tuning in to my four-legged and two-legged patients, being guided by intuition and reading the whole being. Magic is central to my existence and my therapy practice. I see wonder and expect the miracles I witness in everyday life.

Animals & Children See the Truth

Animals and children see the truth, and they do so clearly. Their innocence and uncomplicated lifestyle means they have no façade to uphold or levels of social niceties to aspire to, leaving them free to just be themselves.

I always like to give my animal patients time to get to know me before I presume to examine them, as I know I always feel invaded and my boundaries crossed if a doctor or surgeon does not ask my permission or have the courtesy to explain what he is about to do to me. I always give a little extra time for the animals to smell me and understand me, then I ask their permission and almost always they accept the treatment. Often owners will say how much their dog likes me when they see him cuddling into my leg or rushing in to meet me when they enter my clinic. Although I'm flattered by the thought, I see something quite different, or rather from a different perspective. Yes, they like me, but not for the fluffy reasons their owners believe. What I think is that animals read energy in a similar way to me, which is probably more animal than most humans do, as our ancestors did automatically. They firstly see a warm, loving, unthreatening energy but one which is strong enough for them not to challenge. I also truly believe that they understand that I am a healer.

As people we seem to have largely forgotten that we are still animals and we try to be very sophisticated. The result is that we humans have stopped using - and have therefore lost - many of our animal instincts. However, a few people can still tune in to and utilise these instincts and they are the ones who generally become recognised for their abilities with animals. Certainly I have often tried to examine and explain what it is that I do and I always find it really hard to analyse. There is also a fear that if it is analysed and explained scientifically that I might break the magic and lose the skills!!!

In short I have witnessed me analysing the energy of my patients - be they human or animal - as soon as they come through the door. My general overall sense of that creature is sometimes far from the given presenting problem or history, as I see through to the truth and that is likely to be the thing a patient wants to hide the most. In the wild an animal will try to hide an injury so as not to show their vulnerability - are we humans so different? Many of us subconsciously know what the cause of our symptom is, but it is often a cause that is not easy to change, so we try to bury it behind other things. I'm sure you know someone whose illness is stress-related, caused by a bad marriage or money problems, yet they seem unwilling to do something to change the root cause.

Animals and children are the exception to this, as they tend to live in black or white, ill or well, and do not use the same avoidance tactics in their life stories. Living in the present moment comes naturally to both. Reflecting on the past or drifting into future plans is what most adults do, especially those who have suffered trauma. Most of us spend a large part of our day going over previous conversations or planning what we will do when we win the lottery. Staying present is not easy but that's what less complicated minds do and that's why they are more able to discern truth and genuine emotions from lies.

I stood in the supermarket queue behind a lady with a bright bubbly three-year-old in the shopping trolley. This curly haired toddler talked busily to her mum as the checkout lady put all the groceries through the scanner, smiling at the little girl's antics. The checkout lady, who happened to be blancmange-shaped, was flushed and sweating as she grappled with the bags of spuds she was putting through. Her size compromised her ability to move within her little booth and she seemed wedged in as if made from expanding polystyrene.

"Hello curly" she said to the little girl in the trolley as she came level with her.

"Hello fatty" the child immediately responded, purely from realising they were playing an observation game.

The checkout lady placated the mum's embarrassment and I smiled to watch the child's attention being drawn to the next item of interest, which was the lady at the next till's hair, which was a strange colour... Ever in the present moment, the child was asking questions to help her learn about life, not yet aware of the many falsities we adults employ for all sorts of 'good' reasons.

The Animals in My Life

The land I am now guardian of is beautiful and teeming with wildlife. I stay here not by luck, as many visitors tell me - "Oh you're so lucky to live here" - but by long hard work. I have had no easy journey in this life and everything I have has been gained through blood, sweat and tears. We started refurbishing our farm five years ago and have done it manually brick by brick with only a little help from others. We have chosen to do it as ecologically and environmentally friendly as we can. Beautifully neglected for many years, our hedges remain uncut and are home to hedgehogs, birds, red squirrels and dormice. Early in the morning my first job is to let my chickens out. Each is a character and I am entertained to watch the bantams in their feathery trousers waddle out to greet the day. No-one could ever remain depressed after watching the morning ritual. The cockerel struts and postures, has a peck then a bonk before settling for breakfast - just like most men!

Once the chickens have moved away from the corn and started to peck round the yard the crows move in to grab what they can and this is my favourite time of day. From the nearby rookery they flock down like black bin-bags gusting in the breeze and I love to watch the hierarchical order forming and the antics of their young as they find their place within the group. The crows are the birds of the Morrigan and are one of the protecting forces on my land here. They watch me with their bead-black eyes as they perch round my vegetable patch and no longer fly away when I approach. Guardians of my chicken run, they alert me if a fox is nearby or if one of the farm kittens gets above his station and thinks he might like chicken for supper.

There is a gap at my left side, the place where Tilly, my lurcher friend and co-pilot of the last twelve-and-a-half years would normally be. She moved on after a beautiful death some months ago and no-one else has come into my life to the same level. Like most of the animals who have lived with me, she was a rescue, a Battersea Special, who was three months old. Too crazy for a family to keep as a pet, she was being sent back. "Oh, chuck her in my car, I'll have her" I said to the distressed lady who's horse I had been treating.

Mad as a box of frogs, she jumped round my car and within five minutes had puked and pooed all over it and then spread it all round my car on her feet. She became the most gentle, loving and tactile dog that I have ever met and everyone loved her, but on many occasions created havoc with her crazy antics.

The most memorable was the reputation she got me with the Household Cavalry when I was asked to treat a horse for them just after the 9/11 situation. Security was tight, so many questions were asked prior to my visit. Michelle, the head civilian groom informed me that I would be met at the gate and one of the soldiers would drive my car in.

The date was set for the next Friday. On the Monday before my visit, I was treating a horse whose stables were down a long rough track and on the way home as I bounced along the track, I gagged as my nose was insulted by what I thought was a dog-fart. I glanced into the back seat to see that Tilly had had explosive diarrhoea which had covered the seat and even gone inside the seat-belt clips. With the window wide open and a slightly shamed hound by my side I drove quickly home to clean out my car. As I drove into the yard, my husband met me, saying he had had Michelle from the Household Cavalry on the phone, she had forgotten to ask for my registration number. "Give her yours", I said, "The dog has just shit all over my car". Dave dutifully informed them that it would be a silver estate and not my red Fiesta.

I arrived at Knightsbridge barracks on Friday in my husband's car and could see the security had increased. One soldier, armed and stern-faced, stood beside the driver's door as his colleague searched around the vehicle with a mirror on a stick. Flippantly, I rolled down my window:

"Hello, what are you looking for? Bombs?" I asked appealingly in my best girlie voice. Without smiling or shifting his gaze, this action-man quipped politely:

"No ma'am, dogshit ma'am; your reputation precedes you, ma'am." His colleague grinned as I was ushered through the gates - no-one drove my car in! - but ever since I have been referred to as the 'shit-queen'.

Although mischievous and giving me many a red face, my beautiful girl was kindness itself to both humans and animals. When I entered a familiar yard to treat a horse and saw their normally feisty old collie curled up by the stables, they told me he was going on his last journey to the vet later that afternoon as he had reached the end of his days. My normally daft lurcher, who I always put in the car before I started work on a horse, curled herself round him and lay unmoving until I was ready to leave. As she left him, she licked the top of his head and he closed his eyes. The owner told me later, that when she came to take him to the vet he was already dead and hadn't moved since Tilly left him. Animals are healers too and my girl holds a special place in my heart along with Pal and Treacle my cat.

Treacle died two months after Tilly, at eighteen years old. He came to me at four months old. He had been dumped in a yard where I treated horses and their owner also bred standard-sized Schnauzers. The kitten jumped into the bitch-pen and was pulled apart by the dogs, spilling all his guts. The owner was horrified and got the dogs off, only to be more shocked that he was still alive but in a sorry state. She rushed him to the vet thinking that the kitten would be euthanized, but was told that as they had pulled but not chomped, the dogs had not ruptured the gut.

The vet agreed to clean him up and put it all back in but he said the kitten may be doubly incontinent and may never walk again, in which case bring him back to be put down. Sheepishly she paid the bill, embarrassed that her dogs had caused this little black fluff-ball so much trauma and then she brought him to me for treatment to help him walk again. "You had better leave him with me as this could take a while," I said.

Treacle made a full recovery and lived a long and happy life with no medication or pain. If he needed a chiropractic treatment, he would wait until I was sitting on the toilet and jump on my knee, presenting me with the area to be worked on. He grew to know my every feeling and told me when I was pregnant with my youngest two children before I knew myself. They say witches have black cats as they absorb so much negative energy with no harm to themselves and I could believe that of him. If I was down he would pester and lick me until I smiled, and would then go and lie down. He was a close and dear friend.

In time more animals will find me who may wish to live with me. My husband asked if we can choose our next dog as everything who comes to live here has arrived with a problem or has a bit dropped off! I see hundreds of animals a month in the course of my work but just like humans there are some that I resonate with more readily and they become friends. To become a constant companion, that resonance must be strong.

Many wild creatures share that resonance too, and although they never become constant companions many come into my life and spend some time with me. When these delights happen I look for the message that these animals may bring me and what I can learn from them. Traditions of animal lore describe the characteristics that each species holds and from these many individual messages can be gleaned if one is prepared to see them. A recent experience with a wren was a ten-day intense encounter. The energy was strong although each visit was brief and it earned me the nickname of 'Birdwoman of Alcatraz'.

This little wren would appear in my house - we never did find where it was coming in - and at first it would flutter about slightly worried. We managed to get it into the bathroom which was the best place to confine it and then I opened the window to let it fly out. Over the next few days it came more and more often with many visits per day and eventually became less worried and even quite relaxed in my company, which was unusual for this little bird as wrens are normally quite shy and elusive. Our communication came to a point where I would say to it "Go into the bathroom and I will let you out" at which it would fly up to the bathroom and perch on the towel rail until I had opened the window, occasionally perching on my shoulder as I grappled with the window lever. Each time he would look into my eyes communicating his wisdom to me.

The wren is known as the king of birds the most revered by the Druids, in Gaelic he was called 'Drui-en'. He became thought of as king of birds because of his wisdom and cunning, and the ancient story from the Western Highlands tells us that the birds made this decision. A gathering of all the birds of the air was held to decide who would be the sovereign of the feathered clan. It was decided that the bird who could fly the highest would be crowned king. All the birds thought it would be the Eagle who lazily rode the thermals in the glens and mountains, and could climb so high on these currents of air that he could not be seen from the earth. Confident in his abilities the Eagle flew toward the sun and screeched his power to all the watching eyes. Just then from the feathers on his back out popped the little Wren, who flew above the Eagle's back and shouted to the other birds "Look up and acknowledge your King!"

He shows us that size and strength are not the paths to power, but that wit and gentleness, humility and subtlety are the way to self-realisation. Cunning used with good intent and humour can achieve many tasks.

The word cunning in ancient Scots language had different connotations to the derogatory term used now. It was used to describe the male equivalent to the wise woman. The cunning man was the shaman, the one who wielded wisdom and power. My little wren told me that there are many ways to get out of difficult situations and remaining passive is one way - a way that I am not used to employing. Good advice, that I paid attention to.

Another regular wild visitor here is the barn owl who glides silently over our fields and regularly visits our chicken run in the twilight hours looking for mice and rats. Her startling beauty reminds me of the protection that Owl carries and her wisdom of turning a disadvantage into an advantage is shown in her skill of hunting when other birds have gone to roost. I feel graced by her presence and I stop and watch in reverence and wonder every time I see her.

In contrast to the elegance of this bird are the frogs who inhabit our pond. Regularly seen poised like lumps of mud getting in the way of feet and car-tyres as they make their way back to breed, they risk being squished. My children have become their guardians and 'rescue' as many as they can delivering them safely to the water. At new moon we are graced by their song as they croak and purr like rusty generators as they gather en-masse to lay eggs and start the new generation. In the morning we see the shallows full of tapioca with many of the exhausted frogs basking in the sun as if suffering with a hangover from the wild party the night before. They teach me the joy of transformation and renewal and their sensitivity reminds me to check my feelings towards others.

The joy I feel in observing animals in the wild is beyond expression, they are my teachers and counsellors.

Using the Senses

Magic is life, and life is experienced through our perceptions. But illusions and paradoxes and forgetting and misunderstanding are all part of life too: we need to understand our senses to know what is real and what is not - though I'm not going to define what is 'real' - each of us has to do that for ourselves.

The Sixth Sense

I have spoken about the sixth sense many times, in many ways in previous chapters. But what exactly is it?

In ancient Scottish lore it was a way of describing a person who could commune with the fair folk. These were thought to be the indigenous elders, the ones who were there before the Picts and the Celts. To become a Clan Chief it was believed that they had to marry the land which was embodied in a faery princess. The fair folk had interbred with the incoming peoples and so taught them about the land and magic. So a person who could see and speak with the faeries would have inherited the 'sixth sense'.

More commonly now 'sixth sense' is used to describe a person who has esoteric abilities or a faculty of spiritual perception which is higher and distinct from the five physical senses. These abilities can range widely in skills and can cover a broad spectrum of application. Not everyone practices the same way and there is no right or wrong way. Clairaudients, for example, hear voices which guide them, the most well-known being Joan of Arc, who was given tasks to perform by the Angels. Clairvoyants, on the other hand, have clear inner vision and can see people or events which may be placed at a distance in time or place. Whilst some may use a tool to help them skry, like a crystal ball, others would get the picture straight into their mind's eye.

For a few, the gift comes by being able to see auras, or lay hands on to heal, some talk to spirits or faeries and for others a combination of many skills comes. All are wonderful gifts and should be accepted and respected as that individual's way of working. The ancients of this land were known to revere the different skills within the Orders of Druids. Some were skilled at recalling the histories and singing for the rites. Others could conjure a mist or order the weather or animals to behave a certain way, while some had the gift of sight or herb-lore. All had their place and combined could form a strong force to be reckoned with.

How one chooses a path to follow can happen in lots of different ways. Sometimes it is a case of trial and error, and many cultures or styles need to be sampled to see what feels right. Some individuals may be recognised as having a skill by others and then encouraged to use it. To me, feeling right about it is the crucial part of deciding how to practice, as one should never do anything that feels uncomfortable or unsafe. You may even feel that your path consists of incorporating bits of this and pieces of that, which some teachers are strongly against, but if that is what your path directs, then be true to yourself and follow it.

When I was young, I was progressing nicely on my path, aware that I could contact spirit who guided in my work. I also had an awareness of the spirits around other people and discussed this with a lady who was supposedly skilled as a seer. Hoping for advice on how to progress I explained what I could discern and her reaction was one of shock and discomfort. I was told brusquely that I had to choose between following the path of light or acting as a medium. I was left feeling that I had done something wrong and that spirit contact was a bad thing. It reminded me of my mother's attitude to me in childhood, but fortunately my mentors were able to put the incident into perspective for me. They explained that my contact with spirit WAS working with the light and for good and what I was doing was quite different to the practice of a medium. Working as a medium is not wrong either and there was no problem should I wish to do both, it was not a matter of choosing either/or.

I was lucky to have had clear guidance from no-nonsense elders and was allowed to come to my own decisions with proper informed choice. I suppose that is why it is quite hard for me to categorise what it is that I do, as over time I have become exposed to many aspects of magic. Although I don't 'mix my medicines' as the Native American Elders would say, I do think that a wide experience allows you to be open-minded to varied approaches and different points of view.

The Physical Senses

As adults, we under-use so many of our senses, preferring to stay in our heads following fantasies of one sort or another.

Sight is probably the most overwhelming of our senses. The world we inhabit now continually plays on the power of image and we are exposed daily to visual images to influence what we wear, what we eat, drive, live in, and what to think. Our world is one of straight lines, easy-to-recognise symbols and visible cause-and-effect consequences - and we think we understand how the world works. A lot of the time, we don't actually see what we are looking at! We become blasé and forget that it is all just another fantasy.

Observation played a large part in my magical education: I watched the differences of attitude and approach that the old people had. I have often watched expressions change when I am healing, both in the patients and those looking on. Being aware of another's feelings is not only felt but also observed in their facial expressions and behaviour.

Equally, being able to be honest with yourself and observe your own behaviour objectively, is a really good learning experience. By this I mean examine what you do and how you react, when for example a heated exchange takes place with your work-colleague. How did it make you feel? What did you say and what were you thinking? What did you wish that you had said and done, when you mulled it over later? Then, what was it that stopped you doing that ideal action at the time?

That ability to break things down and examine them honestly helps you to get to know yourself so if you start making excuses, ask yourself why. What are you hiding? Only when you are able to be brutally honest about your own weaknesses can you begin to change them. Observation is the start of that change.

ഒ ⊙ ര

Our sense of smell is underestimated as a source of information in our daily lives. Too often that information is lost behind a wall of perfume that can cover up human odours. Fear and illness both have a distinct smell and other pheromones released in any exchange are subtle and can be lost in the artificial smells ladled on in the shape of deodorant, body spray, aftershave, hairspray, shampoo and perfume - not to mention soap powder and fabric conditioner. Our homes are no longer allowed to smell of us but are expected to have the neutral whiff of cleanliness.

My husband, Dave, has often watched me treat and has commented on how often I will smell an animal, either its breath or coat, and remark on its state of health judged by the information that gives me. I do this subconsciously and I am told that I rely on smell to influence my description of things. I know that I have said in the past that I drive with my car window open so I can smell the land I am crossing and get to know it. I find it hard to understand how others can say they know a place without the smell - it tells me so much. I discover things like how dry or damp the soil is, what vegetation grows there and how healthy that vegetation is. I can smell habitation and know if they burn fires. Bodies of water sing to me and I guess in days gone by that would have been a sense that would have led me to drinking water if I had been travelling or herding animals.

I spoke earlier about the sense of smell being linked via the pituitary and pineal glands to the intuition. It would seem that modern-day humans spend an awful lot of money covering up their smells. Could they be afraid that others will smell the truth of their fear?! That would tell me that we are also blotting out our abilities to intuit. I would urge everyone to have a day without false scent and get to know your own smell, you might be surprised at what it will tell you about yourself!

$$\text{\textpbrk} \odot \text{\textpbrk}$$

Who do you touch? In my life, touch is what earns my living. As a doctor of chiropractic my sense of touch has been honed to detect subtle misalignments of the skeleton and tightness of the ligaments. I am sensitive to pain and organic change on the skin and I use my skills of touch to soothe, ease and comfort my patients. Many of my elderly patients will tell me, when I massage them, that it is the first time they have been touched since their husband died twenty years ago.

Since we have stopped living in tribal groups we have reduced how much we touch one another and laws of political correctness have now made that more obvious. The comfort of a cuddle is limited to partners or our children, a gift only rarely given to a friend. Human touch can mean so much to someone injured or distressed. If you think about it, we are still animals, so we should be grooming each other, checking for nits and integrating as friends to reaffirm group bonds. Instead we visit hairdressers at great expense and get groomed by someone who offers superficial niceties and would be embarrassed if we groaned in pleasure and asked them to "do that again"!

Time has also altered our sense of taste. From bland subsistence foods we have moved to expect rich, tasty food, sometimes spicy, often sweet, and good quality wines on a daily basis. The supermarkets have thrived on our need to have luxury at our fingertips and fruit and veg all year round. Fast foods appeal to our need for 'tasty' by producing salty processed burgers with cheese. Many food manufacturers manipulate their products to include artificial chemicals that make our brains crave for more.

Too seldom do we sit at our tables and celebrate what we eat and rarely do we eat slowly enough to savour the flavour and nourishment in every bite. Do you bless your food before you eat it? Do you give thanks to the plants and animals on your plate? I do when I take time to remember, but like everyone else on a busy work day I am guilty of shoving in a sandwich from the petrol garage without any thought other than 'I hope the person who made this washed their hands first and didn't have that bug that's going round!'.

In ceremonies and rituals we can still have the opportunity to experience wonderful, or sometimes weird tastes. A ceremonial mouthful of water can be the most exquisite thing you have ever tasted after a long ritual or a fast. Occasionally herbs are used to help on the shamanic journey and some people travel to the jungles to sample ayahuasca, a vomit-inducing drug which brings hallucination but is also said to aid the inner vision. In Britain, similar poisonous herbs were used in the same way, not only as smokes and herbal drinks but as ointments. Witches' flying ointments were hallucinogenic and were rubbed on the temples, wrists and broom handles. Masturbation against the rods of wood massaged the genitals against the ointment which was absorbed into the system quickly and created the vision and the effect of flying. The application this way prevented vomiting and gave lesser after-effects. The most commonly drunk herbs to aid vision were wormwood tea and certain mushroom soups, which are highly poisonous but used in the right quantities gave the desired effects, and are still used to this day.

$$\mathfrak{SO} \odot \mathfrak{CR}$$

Sound would seem to be the least employed sense in the course of magic. Over the last fifty years ambient sound has increased. Our ears today are bombarded with the constant noises of traffic, planes, factory noise, radio and TV. Our homes have the whirr of machinery in the shape of fridge-freezers, computers and central heating boilers.

Studies have been made of birds who live in towns, who now have to sing much louder to attract a mate as they would be drowned out by the background noise of vehicles. This lack of quiet must affect humans too - government research shows that people crave peace and quiet in the countryside. Silence is a rare and wonderful thing!

Music is used to entertain us, but we don't often think of it being used to soothe us as it would have been used by our mothers when we were babies. In some parts of the world shamen still use music and chanting to heal with, or retrieve lost souls. In our churches today the hymns sung are viewed as poetical niceties while their original purpose was to induce the trance-like state and help us to enter the spirit mind to be able to commune closer with our God. Places of worship were built and designed in past times as cathedrals to enhance sounds. Research claims that Stonehenge has had the stones cut and edged to create surfaces to guide sound, so it may be that we have continued to use these skills in our communal places of worship that were recognised from the roundhouse roofs. It creates a very magical atmosphere to sit in a roundhouse after dark, lit only by the fire and some candles, and chant. The smoke from the fire, infused with herbs, hangs in the roof-space. Drumming and chanting in these surroundings transports the psyche to a different level.

When we look at modern churches they tend to have similar qualities in that they are generally big and dark, only allowing light in through coloured windows. We sit there cut off from the outside world and experience the smell of incense and the sound of chanting. This is designed to induce the trance-like state and enable our communion with the higher spirits. But how many people enter a church and are aware of this?

Historically, sound has played a bigger part in our lives although very little evidence is left to support this. Fragments of writing in the Bible and other historical documents tell us how sound was used as a weapon. 'The horns brought down the walls of Jericho...' - is this a metaphor or a reality? We have been left tales of war-harps - great stringed monsters which gave off a sound so deadly that the enemy would retreat. Was this fear of a scary inhuman sound or were they producing sound waves and patterns that could create physical damage and hurt the eardrums? It is told that in Scotland the bodhran, an instrument of music, a skin drum beaten with a short stick, was developed from the sounds created by warriors banging on hide and wood shields with their swords to build up the adrenalin for war and intimidate their foes. We know now about sonics and how soundwaves travel and so it is quite feasible that intuitively our ancestors did too, and used it in the forms they had available to them.

I personally believe that the great monuments that are found in this world like Stonehenge and the Great Pyramids were built using sound to help transport the stone. Little evidence is available to support the idea that the conventional building techniques that we know of today were capable of achieving the accuracy and timescales that these megaliths were built in. As children we used to play a levitation game where a group of us would put a finger under a person who was lying down or sitting on a chair. We would all chant and concentrate then after a little time we would lift that person and they would seem as light as a feather. A child's game with little substance, but where did the idea come from? - and it always worked. Is it not possible that great blocks of stone could have been lifted in the same way? Certainly the likes of 'Time Team' have not found evidence to support the historian's proposed engineering theories although they have mocked up what they thought must have been used.

I remember the old black and white films that were on TV in my childhood, where Humphrey Bogart was doing something hot and sweaty in the jungle. He was accompanied by a whimpering woman with a great figure and a shirt that was just too tight. She didn't shed a bead of sweat and her makeup remained perfect. The whole story was probably pointless but the thing that sticks in my mind were their teams of African slaves who chanted some diaphragm-pulsing sounds as they pulled heavy weights. I have no doubt that these chants were authentic although what they were saying I couldn't guess at, but the resonance in my body made the hairs on the back of my neck stand up.

It feels unclear to me whether this form of chanting was to coordinate the rhythm of pulling as depicted in these old films or whether, like my childhood game, could have been a tool for levitation.

Chanting has many purposes and levitation may have been one. In war, chants provided a remote threat which showed the strength and togetherness of the opposing group. We can still witness a remnant of this on the rugby fields today when the New Zealand All-Blacks team performs the haka. I was lucky enough to be at Murrayfield for a Scotland versus England rugby match some years ago when the flagging Scottish team was lifted by the overwhelming singing of the crowd as 'Flower of Scotland' reverberated through the stands. They could not fail to win after their souls were energised and their bodies roused by so many supporting voices. 'Flower of Scotland' was adopted as the national anthem a short while after this, replacing 'Scotland the Brave' which no-one could sing.

Modern technology is now exploring the idea of sound to heal with, as they can view the effect that soundwaves have on the body. This is supporting the work that shamen have done for thousands of years, but if science can prove it, then suddenly it's authentic. Keening for the dead not only carried the soul on its journey but eased the suffering of the loved ones left behind.

An American scientist I spoke with some years ago was using this same theory of sound healing with the study she was doing with dolphins. She was exploring the fact that so many people are healed by swimming with dolphins.

Her idea was that this may come about because the dolphins scan the humans with their sonar and look for the missing or damaged octave. She told me that the dolphins have hollow teeth which gave them to ability to gauge, monitor and produce these sounds. They offer that missing sound by producing the note with their ultrasonics which harmonised the body's frequencies and produced the healing effect.

There is so much we have yet to understand about communication between animals like whales and elephants, dolphins and insects, or even our domestic pets whose ranges of hearing and producing sounds differs to ours. How much have we forgotten that our ancestors understood and worked with daily?

In the still places left on our Earth nature feels serene and glorious - could she be breathing a sigh of relief to be away from interfering noise? Treat your senses and relax in a quiet sanctuary where you can indulge each sense with Mother Earth's gift.

Old Magic in Everyday Life

The idea of magic being something that is separate from everyday life - known to the magicians but not the ordinary people - still slows down our recognition that it is here, now, of the Earth and Universe, all around us, and perhaps most essentially, in us.

Beginnings and Endings

My mobile phone has just beeped at me to let me know I have a message. The title says 'Hi Granny' and a video of my new grandson coos and goos at me and makes me smile. Then I ask myself, how can I have written all this criticism of modern technology when I too enjoy the perks of modern life. As a mother and grandmother now, I reflect back to my own mother's and grandmother's lives and note the differences. I certainly would not like to go back to washing sheets in a boiler and wringing them out in a mangle!

We will never return to times gone by - we will progress to new times where there will be good and bad - but if we can hold on to the values of many of the old ways and view our technology as convenience tools and not essentials we are less likely to lose the skills and reverence for this world we live in.

The old magic of faerie is lost in the mists of time, surfacing only in quiet, magical places to those with eyes to see it. Christianity has pushed the worship of Earth as Goddess into the mists and now technology is pushing Christianity and all other religious belief systems into the mists. The reality for the majority in the developed world now revolves around TV and regular worship of the nightly soaps operas. The lifestyles watched are emulated and revered, creating values based on pretence and drama. I couldn't believe my ears when visiting a patient who said "Ssshh! They're sleeping!" as he watched the inmates of Big Brother!

Life continues to change and the media, while holding the attention of the majority via soap and chat shows, have the ability to prepare the masses for the major forthcoming upheavals. The coverage of the financial changes as the big banks started to crumble and the credit crunch took hold influenced the public's reactions both good and bad. More regularly, we see reports on peak oil and climate change and the coming changes in agriculture which will affect us all. More programmes about self-sufficiency and growing your own veg are available to watch and the interest shown in these is a gauge of the public's awareness of the changes ahead. The Times newspaper reported that the National Trust is planning to turn the grounds of stately Homes into allotments, encouraging everyone to plant their own vegetables.

These changes ARE the apocalyptic predictions of 2012 given by many ancient cultures. The Mayans spoke of the End Times - the end of an era - and it will certainly be the end of an era when oil runs out and the change will start as soon as it becomes more scarce and the price escalates. The skills are lost which could take us back to ploughing with horses like old Campbell did, anyway today few have the dedication or stamina to work as he did.

We cannot go back, the skills are lost and there aren't enough trained heavy horses. Now we must use our scientific knowledge, our technical abilities AND the old respect for the planet as a living entity - our providing mother - to take us to a better future.

During these transitions many will suffer and feel unable

to cope with the changes but I look forward to it and long to sit on a hillside and hear silence again when no planes are flying or motorways lined with cars. I will enjoy teaching my grandsons how to plant and grow and be able to help them learn some of the old skills. They may never need them, but if they do, they will have that knowledge. My daughters have been taught how to spin, weave and knit - they may choose not to but if they ever need to they can - or if some modern technique needs to be developed it can be done with a basic understanding of the fundamentals. My granddaughters will be shown the places where they may contact the faeries and will be taught the correct way to do so. They will be shown how to respect the trees and understand their properties and lore as I was shown. I hope they will be able to hear the trees speak back to them.

The path of magic has no signposts or directions visible to the modern eye. Guidance can come from those who have travelled those ways before but mainly it can only be found when one slows down to look and listen and then when one is ready to find it. True magic won't be found on a computer screen or in a book - it will be found in the dirt of your garden or in a nearby hedge. Like the children who believe they can drive a racing car or kill a terrorist because they can do it on an interactive game station, confusion and separation arises if you learn magic from a book. Instead, go out into the wild places and the stone circles - just be there still and quiet - it may take time, but you are much more likely to achieve true magic that way.

You can guarantee it will not be instant like a lesson in Hogwarts, it will take you years, so start right away. The old Druid teachings said 'Look for that which repeats again and again, for that is the message given by the gods for you to learn'. Self-development requires that you are honest with yourself and work on your weak points, and that is the same in magic and any energy work. Self-delusion is a common fault readily witnessed at any psychic fair or shamanic conference.

I don't believe you have to go through hell to find your true path, although it would appear that that is how many do find it. Perhaps trauma in your life brings you down to earth and helps to put things into perspective more quickly. Unable to be bought in a shop, the sacred truth of magic is frustratingly out of reach for those used to the instant gratification of a credit card purchase. This makes its worth that bit more special. Get to know your own skills and allow yourself to be drawn where your gut feelings lead you and explore these places. Soon you will become aware of where your own interests and skills lie.

When we lived in small villages everyone was aware of the skills of others who lived there. I remember a lad in a village I lived in, who was not very bright and could have been thought of unkindly as the village idiot. Instead his skills had been noted by the old men and he was given jobs that suited him. Soon everyone knew that if you had something needing to be calved, foaled, lambed or whelped, Robin was your man. He could dig a Jack Russell out of a rabbit hole accurately and never lost a dog, and he could skin a carcass quicker than anyone I've ever seen. Recognised and mentored in these skills, he had a role within the community and was valued as a worthy contributor in that village. All skills have a worth and even if yours are different from those of others, be proud of them and stand in your own place, knowing your own abilities.

ॐ ☉ ॐ

Over time I have grown used to my skills and accept even the odd visions that come to me as things for me to witness, not always mine to act on. When a premonition comes to me now I always ask if I need to do anything about it, as some things are not mine to change. Some people may think that a cop-out but if I were to get upset with every vision I'm given I would be a neurotic wreck very quickly. Many visions come in daydreams or meditations and others during sleep as dreamtime visions (as opposed to dreams).

One of these dreamtime visions took me to my grandmother's house and I relived the situation when she gave me the crystal ball. I could smell the house and observe details of a house long forgotten. I was reminded again of the whole situation and so next time I spoke to my Mum on the phone I described what I had seen as if in a dream. Then I mentioned that what happened next was when she had come into the room and had witnessed Granny giving me the crystal ball.

Suddenly I was cut off - so I redialled. "Hi Mum, I wa…" again cut off. After the fifth attempt I gave up realising she didn't want to discuss it. A couple of weeks later we spoke again and I dared not mention the dream until later. When I brought it up I asked what had happened to the crystal ball. "Oh, all that stuff in the cupboard was thrown out when the house was cleared".

Then she said - "You know I tried to keep you from it all but you found your way to it anyway!".

"Why does it scare you so much?"

"Oh it's all just rubbish and I don't want to go to Hell for thinking about it."

No more was mentioned but a change in our relationship started from that moment. Nowadays, although still sceptical, she will ask for a treatment or a remedy for aches or ills that she would never have dared to do before. Time is a healer and she has probably mellowed with age, but we stay off the subject of magic. In a way, the dream legitimised my knowing, even though she dismissed it.

$$\text{ʂͻ}\odot\text{ͼʅ}$$

I entered into the world of research with a desire to show the scientific community that Healing - often considered as whacky as dowsing - had a real effect and was a real process. I had met a woman who was using a machine called a PIP-scanner - a modern version of Kirlian photography showing a computer-generated image of the aura. She was interested to see what she could monitor when I did healing on phantom limb pain with amputees, a thing that I was well-known for success with. We were also both interested to know what changes could be seen at each phase of my normal treatment with animals.

My usual routine was to watch the animal move after I have taken details of its medical history. Next I would palpate the bones seeking subtle misalignments that cause pain, movement problems or other impairments of function. Then I treat these misalignments with chiropractic manipulation and a full body massage focussing on any soft tissue areas which were particularly problematic. That would then normally be followed up with some healing - balancing the energy bodies and reinforcing any of the main problem areas already worked on.

To be able to analyse all this scientifically we needed the machine to be the most efficient it could be. "We would need a bald horse", she laughed, "otherwise the electrical patterns within the hair might affect the reading". "Don't worry, I will arrange it" - nothing was going to stop me proving that this could work. I had arranged to work on a friend's hunter who was used to being clipped - he was not quite so used to being stripped with skinning blades. But I produced my bald horse on a pleasantly warm day, and everything was set up to run these tests.

To make it all scientifically correct, the area was cleared of anything that might affect the readings. The lady with the technology sat on the rafters of the barn looking down on the horse's back and tuned in her machine before we started, to give us a baseline reading. On the screen a multi-coloured computer generated image could pick up the lines of energy, that acupuncturists would call meridian lines, and we could clearly see the energy of his aura pulsing gently around him in varying shades of greens and blues. Areas of discomfort were shown in pink to red colours making positive correlations with the palpation of misalignments I was finding in his spine prior to adjusting them. Once treated chiropractically another image was taken showing that the pink and red areas had reduced and the colours in the aura changed. Massage treatment followed on next and then another image taken showed yet more change where the pink and red areas had diminished and the aura expanded in gentle colours around the horse.

"Keep going", the technician shouted, "I'm going to let the camera run - go right into the healing section", so I tuned into the horse and let my focus drop into my solar plexus, slowing my pulse and therefore moving my brainwaves into healing mode. "Jesus Christ!" was the scream from the rafters "Wow, just keep going!!!" What the playback showed was that as soon as I tuned into healing mode a shaft of silvery light came down through my head. My hands, which were included in the picture, which had shown the meridian lines of my hands and arms, had changed to look like I was wearing silver oven-gloves. Then silver flowed from my hands and dissipated along the horse's spine. All areas of pink and red changed to greens and blues, the horse's aura expanded to include yellow and the whole auric body was edged with a golden tinge. She couldn't believe what she had seen and played it over and over again. I was delighted to have what I thought was indisputable evidence that healing energy was a real thing and a tangible catalyst to change within the body.

I wrote up all my evidence, careful to translate it into science-speak as my professor had explained that qualitative evidence was less acceptable than quantitative evidence, and therefore what I presented must be very concise, tight and persuasive. My first draft was well-received, highly marked and enthusiastically praised - but then "Is this piece of equipment validated?" I was asked over the phone. "No?" "Then the research is not acceptable."

I contacted the technician, then Harry Oldfield, the originator of the equipment, and he put me on to Julian Kenyon in Southampton, who put me on to another researcher who had validated the machine. "You will have to send him an email" I was told, "as he is in the middle of the jungle but I don't know when he will pick it up". He did get back to me very quickly but all was looking gloomy for my timescale and validation requirements and in the end, feeling depleted and disappointed I decided to let it all go. I was devastated.

Full of anger and frustration I found it hard to understand that other people were not amazed at what had been shown on the PIP-scanner. My husband - my warrior and my anchor - watched my pain and as always put into words the clarification that helped me find peace. He described it as being like two islands with a bridge between, one which held the healers who worked with energy, magic, and unseen skills, and the other which held the scientists. He said I was standing with the scientists saying the answer is over there and trying to persuade them to cross the bridge, when really I should have been standing with the healers waving over to the scientists saying 'the answer is over here when you are ready to come over the bridge to find it'.

This gave me the permission I needed to let it all go and stand in my own space and just work with what I understood. It also gave me more confidence to speak openly about the healing work because now other people had actually seen it and although I had always believed it, the conditioning from childhood that I was telling lies still made me doubt my own abilities on occasion.

Although all the wonderful evidence is still there - stored - perhaps to be brought out again another day, it was enough just to do it to take me into a better place of understanding my own strengths and weaknesses. Perhaps the world was not yet ready for such obvious proof - and perhaps I needed to do more work on my ego to lower my sights to something more achievable.

Magic Hidden

I sit here today in my home on the Isle of Wight looking out at brilliant blue skies and feel spring in the air. The buzzards are wheeling overhead calling out for new partners and down the valley I can see some white triangular sails against the blue sea as people are venturing out on the water again. I'm reminded by the abundance of beauty of my land that this country was referred to in ancient times as the land of milk and honey because of its lush green pastures and vegetation. Now our milk industry is falling into tatters and a few large dairies take the place of several small ones. In 2008 Britain lost a third of its honeybee population and the cause is as yet unknown. Some say it could have been the weather, while others think the increase in mobile phone masts, crop-sprays or verroa disease are the cause. The truth is, no-one yet knows as until recently little money was put up by the Government to research into bees, their diseases and worth to our farming industry. Our politicians who sit in London offices are so far removed from the land that their decision-making focuses around financial balances and often forgets the grassroots connection to our food sources.

Many inherent understandings have not been passed on to the younger generations because while obvious to those still working on the land, they have held no value to those who's lives have taken them away from the country. Some years ago I was following the hunt on foot as two horses in my care were out on the field. It was a beautiful morning and the pace was fast and everyone was moving on quickly. I managed to get a lift with one of the old farmers who was following in his Landrover and he had lived and worked in this area all his life. As the field and followers headed right at a T-junction he turned left. "Where are you going?" I asked.

"They will head round the far side of the copse, but they will wheel back in this direction in a bit." He said confidently.

"How do you know? I asked hesitantly, not wanting to seem ignorant.

"Because that's the way the wind's blowing, and Charlie Fox will head that way and double back on himself!"

I was clearly shown that the inherent understanding of hunting was held by these old men who understand the land, the animals and their reactions to the weather, more than the red-coated huntsmen or the wealthy horse-owners who followed for a jolly time.

It is so easy to see where and how magic has become lost from our lives so that many of us have become disconnected. Sometimes it is even hard to recognise it as old magic when it is right under our noses, if our eyes are not open to see it.

ॐ ⊙ ॐ

So where can we see magic in our everyday lives?

Alongside the growing numbers of people who, usually in the form of big industry, damage and neglect our world, are the growing numbers of those who care. Those who see that there has got to be another way, bring a balance by opposing the mass destruction for short-term gain, the greed and materialism that has been the trend for too many years. The growing resurgence of the animistic belief systems, where the love of the earth and nature are revered and spirit is seen in rocks, trees and all of the creatures of this world, is replacing many of the religious systems which have shown themselves hypocritical in recent years. This growing body of people who show spiritual interest in the earth are rediscovering some of the old magic and refinding lost ways.

Much of the old magic remains in place, undisturbed and unchanged for hundreds of years. It is often found in unexpected places, not hidden away but equally not explicitly explained. These covert mysteries were alluded to in Dan Brown's book 'The DaVinci Code' and although it was written as a thriller novel, many truths lie behind the fiction. A lot of the world's mysteries are concealed in the vaults of religious bodies and kept from the public gaze 'for our own sakes', with the excuse that if brought out into the open, it could fall into the wrong hands and be damaging to the people. Some mysteries are allowed to be in the public domain but are encouraged to be seen as trivial tourist interests. This keeps the power hidden but also prevents any ridicule or criticism for following magic that might be thrown at those performing the rituals.

The most obvious magical markers are the remaining megaliths like Stonehenge where thousands of tourists visit each year. It stands alone open to discussion and suggestion of its purpose and is the root of much argument as to its history. Another major tourist site also holds old magic at its core, although it is a bit more esoteric. That place is the Tower of London.

Like many major buildings of importance, it was built on an old site of energetic relevance and that place was called White Hill. This forms a line with Parliament Hill and is the mid-summers' day azimuth - the line on which the sun rises. This is now the site of White Tower in the Tower of London and is the resting place of Bran the Blessed's head. Much myth and legend surrounds this mystery and like all the old tales there are many different versions and beliefs.

The legend from the Welsh Triads tells us that Bran was the King of Britain. His name Bran translated as crow or raven. His pedigree made him a powerful sovereign, respected throughout for his desire to protect the lands. His dying wish was that his head was cut off and buried on White Hill facing France and as long as it lay undisturbed Britain would remain safe from invasion. Bran is represented by the ravens that he was named for and the legend says 'If the Tower of London ravens are lost or fly away, the Crown will fall and Britain with it.'

Arthurian tales talk about the head being dug up by King Arthur who claimed that he was the only guardian of this country. As far as I am aware the head remains buried in its original site. What interests me is that fact that Bran is represented by the ravens that our Government keeps at the Tower. There have been times when there have been no ravens at the Tower, the last being just before World War Two. Then London was bombed and the ravens have since been brought back. They are maintained by the Yeoman Warder Raven-master, a man employed by the Government to care for these birds either to ensure the legend is upheld or to act as a tourist attraction - or both! The birds are protected by royal decree upheld since the time of Charles the Second who ruled that at least six birds be kept at the Tower. This is old magic still upheld by our Government and Royal Family for what I believe is their belief in the power of this old talisman.

Other old talismen can be found in the shape of Sheela-Na-Gig and Green Man images seen in old churches in these lands. Churches were built on pagan sites of worship - areas of land energy - and these talismen were built into the modern building either as a mark of respect or fear of the old religion, or by the stone masons who probably still followed the old way.

Sheela-Na-Gig is the symbol of fertility and protection and is portrayed by a female image holding an abnormally large vulva wide open and pulled into the lozenge shape indicative of older Neolithic goddess symbols, and is usually carved from stone and positioned over a doorway. The image resembles the *cailleach*, the hag of Celtic lore, who I think invites one to step over the threshold into the female wisdom and power within! - the ancient, knowing, raw power of the old woman - not the sexual reproductive power associated with beauty.

Sheela-Na-Gig is usually accompanied by the Green Man, another powerful guardian who balances her female energy with his male energy. He is depicted in many shapes and forms, sometimes horned as *cernunnos* or Herne the Hunter, but usually a leaf-encrusted head with the human face peering through and is positioned on the buildings as guardian of the place.

Neither of these symbols are pretty or attractive and so would not be put there as decorative fancies: therefore they fulfilled another purpose. That purpose was magical protection and recognition of magical power and again these symbols remain in churches today where political correctness has not yet removed what could be seen as a distasteful image.

As spring approaches, many English village pubs celebrate the warmer weather and we see people begin to sit outside as the umbrellas go up and the tables appear in the beer gardens again. We all enjoy sitting having a pint and watching the Morris Men dance symbolising the summer to come. But do you see an eccentric English folk dance or do you see the underlying symbolism and energetic awakening when the dancers shake the bells and dance in spirals or do the footwork that has deeper meaning? That deeper meaning hails from the ancient ritual dances done to awaken the land energy and to make the patterns on the land associated with power which would help to create the magic the shamen were aiming to perform. Mostly these would be fertility rites, ensuring the health of the people, the herds they hunted and the vegetation that sustained them all.

Many of the fertility rituals were built round respecting the land as Goddess and Her human representative would be a woman of faerie ancestry. She would be mated with the year king who was usually a prized warrior or hunter and his choosing would involve a ritual killing of a deer with his bare hands. The stags antlers would be worn by the chosen man during his ceremony with the queen and their mating would ensure the fertility of the tribe for another year. Remnants of this type of festival can still be seen today during events like the Abbotts Bromley Horndance. It takes place around Lughnasad and involves six deer men, a fool and a hobby horse. The deer antlers are kept in the church! And from that place they dance and perform to the music of a melodeon as they journey round the farms and pubs of the village ending at the village centre.

The hobby horse is another potent symbol of old magic - Penglaze, Pale Mary, the Obby Oss are the main characters within some old ritualistic dances. Some of the dances are performed with a real horse skull being used as the main part of the costume. Although history tells us that these dances started in the 1200's, that probably means that that is when there is first written evidence of them as they have been around much longer. Could they link to the stories of the shamen flying on their spirit horses to the underworld and hail back to tribal times?

Our beloved Santa Claus comes from similar shamanic stories of the old north. Some tales tell of his red and white coat being blood-covered reindeer skins after the cull and that the gifts he brings are meat and the heart, liver and kidneys, which would have to be eaten quickly as they would not store but were a delicacy often gifted by a hunter to those in favour. Other tales describe the red and white of the coat symbolising the fly agaric mushroom used by Siberian shamen to induce the trance flight. So tied to the herds of reindeer as a way of life, they observed that these beasts also ate the mushrooms and so the shamen would drink the deer urine to obtain the hallucinogenic effect while reducing the danger to themselves. When in the trance state they would leave their bodies and travel out of the skin tents through the smoke holes to begin their astral flight. Then they would return the same way, which has given us the story of Santa coming down the chimney.

Much of the original reasonings and rituals of these old ways have been lost with the traditional stories and verbal teachings. Changed over time with the new story-tellers flourish of embellishment or the words mispronounced with the change of accent, many traditional customs and sayings have lost their roots. My granny had a favourite saying which had come down her mother-line to my mother which was 'Ne'er cast a cloot till May is oot'. It was said to us as children when we objected to wearing the layers of scratchy vests and woollen hats that were the standard clothing in the Scotland of my childhood. The saying meant 'Never take off any (cloots) clothes until the blackthorn has flowered and month of May has passed' inferring that you might get chilled and unwell if you did. I was interested to hear this linked to the English saying of 'A pinch and a punch, the first of the month' (which I had never heard in Scotland) by the presenters of a children's TV programme who described quite authoritatively that the Scottish version was 'Never cast a clout till May is out'. This they explained meant 'Never give a clout or a punch...!' It let me see clearly how easily things get twisted.

How many times have you heard someone say 'I'm sure this or that will happen... ... ... touch wood'. Christianity would have us believe that it comes from early pilgrims bringing back supposed pieces of Jesus' cross, which they would touch for luck. Actually, touchwoods hail back to times when Britain was a forested land and tree lore was much more understood and followed. Runic staves were used as an oracle and were made from our native trees, each of which had its own properties. To 'touch wood' meant to touch the lucky rune usually worn on a thong round the neck. So the next time you say it - think about it's meaning!

$$\text{ꍏ} \odot \text{ꍏ}$$

One of my dogs 'wuffs' which makes me jump out of my skin. Settled here at my garden table and lost in the thoughts of my writing, I could be lifetimes away. Mother Nature's arms, wrapped around me, give me the peace and space to think and the gentle Sunday morning pulse lets me drift into a quieter time when life moved more slowly.

The smell of coffee makes me turn and look as Dave comes out with a new steaming mug and a plate of hot toast, which he leaves beside me. With a squeeze of my shoulder he disappears back inside - as ever my warrior respecting my space and my connection to the energies. The dogs wag their tails and wander back inside with him. I think of my warrior-lover, the smell of hot coffee, the smell of the land, the sound of the wren peeping... ... ...

Journey

72 BC, Valley of the Ashes, Isle of Wight

I watched as the rain ran in rivulets down my cleavage and the inside of my naked thigh. The sky had hung heavy for days just leaking enough moisture to seep into the hearts of the bravest and dampen their fire. Water dripped off the dark grey mane of my mare and ran in darkening streaks down her shoulder. She shifted her weight, oblivious to the gathering fear and the gathering storm. She knew to save her energy, as I did, until it was really needed.

The smir cast the distant hills into grey nothing and the open moor before us ghosted anything solid into fearful shadows. The warriors grew impatient as they could not see the enemy and it was hard to keep the anger up without a foe to face. I thought "Their priests have done well to cast this screen".

I checked again, my shield was solid, my hand through the grip, the leather thongs wrapped round my wrist, snaking up my arm beside the red morphic horse tattooed on my forearm and thumb. My sword sat gently in my right hand, weighted evenly with the butt so it felt light as a feather, the mackerel markings in the dark metal proving the skill of the smith. It was made by my grandmother and laced with her magic - it would not fail me.

From my right a small brown streak darted towards me and landed with a flick and a bob on my mare's neck. The wren tipped his beady black eye towards me. "Hail, King of Birds - you bring me a message?" I asked. He looked deep into my soul, his courage warming mine and with another bob and flick of his tail he was gone into the bramble thicket.

The drumming started and at it's first heartbeat, a collective intake of breath as the gathered crowd felt the reality of us being there. The young men and women roared their fight into the fog to release their tension and I watched as the elders exchanged glances and rechecked who was by their sides. A last loving glance was thrown in front of fear to family and lovers as the war band started to move downhill into the swirling grey.

My mare's warm damp hair rubbed against my thighs, her strength reassuring, the scent of her sweat soothing my churning gut. The drum beats following us grew faster and wilder as the first of the group reached the lower ground. Amidst the quickening music a solid beat of sword on shield was initiated by the older men and the roars of the young ceased. This was as it had been foretold round the fire.

Then it came - the inevitable stench of voided bowels as the mist revealed the dark mass of the enemy. Still and silent like a brooding demon they sat and waited on the other side of the valley. Our gallant young warriors puked and peed like babes in arms and many keeled - rubber-kneed at the sight. Heartbeats pounded as fear rushed like a tidal wave over our war-band - we were out-numbered three to one. The horses screamed as mouths were jabbed and legs tightened round their bellies. The wheels of the cart creaked more desperately as the ponies picked up the sense of urgency and pulled against their shafts.

My steady grey mare flicked her ears back and listened to my breathing - still even - as I dropped my senses into my solar plexus. I calmed my mind and focussed my hate on the other side. Who would it be that would reap my wrath? - pick three and then go for the strongest.

There he was - big, bawdy, loud and ugly - his fair hair with warrior braids either side - our eyes locked in hatred. I knew he had seen me although he was still too far away to see clearly but I sensed he had marked me as I had him.

He too was an experienced fighter. To his right a woman - his woman - she would fight viciously when I killed him. To his left a trusted friend - a yes man - weak. He would die willingly. I breathed deeply and my mare threw her head up - she knew it was almost time.

As one the shield-beaters and drummers stopped. In the pregnant silence, prayers were thought and weapons checked. Then the bubble of stillness burst as the foot soldiers ran forwards shouting - the energy of youth and bravado exploded from both sides to meet with a clash of metal and the thudding of swords on shields, shields on bodies and bodies on earth.

Behind them the older steadier warriors moved in, killing rhythmically, fighting shoulder to shoulder with trusted peers and the young fell to their experience. The smell of acid from spilled guts and the sweet sticky congealing of blood set the horses on edge. They stamped and fidgeted as their fear mixed with that of their rider ready to ignite the third phase of the battle.

The carts moved first, their creaking wheels gathering to a high-pitched squeal as they wheeled round the outside of the heaving throng to allow fresh warriors to leap off and join the battle, coming in from the edges. The charioteer's skilled eyes had already picked out a route where his cart could run safely. He had also identified who he could pick up on his way back and deliver them to safety behind the battle ground. His steady hands held the feisty ponies and his encouraging words would drive them at this pace all day - finally collecting the dead and wounded.

The screams and grunts of the fight grew - my mouth had gone dry. I was aware of the ugly brute focussing on me and my hatred grew colder than the metal of my sword.

A gut-trembling guttural roar left my body as the mare and I as one, plunged forward leading the riders in from the rear. We crashed through the battle hacking and slicing at heads and shoulders, faces and arms as they came into vision. The crack of bone under hoof sickened the senses as we made our way across the fight aiming at the mounted warriors coming towards us. Guided by my legs, my mare's head was free to snake and bite at approaching danger. Knowing I would stick with her she plunged and lashed out at both human and horse, deeply engrossed in her own battle. Her reasons for doing it no more deeply pledged than mine - she was good at it - and together we were a ferocious dance.

Then we were face to face - the fair-haired bear - bigger and uglier close-up everything I detested in a human and his rancid scent told me of his fear. "Steady mare" I eased her back - brought her back with me. Her awareness had to be on this man, he was both fierce and scared, a dangerous combination. His arms were strong, his reach long, we would have to move round him quickly.

His horse lunged into us, knocking my mare sideways - his huge sword came down heavy on my shield. It embedded into the leather and wood and I felt the tendons in my shoulder strain but the sword was held just long enough for my mare to twist to his shield side pulling him with us. Off balance just for a second it allowed my my sword arm to come up and under, splitting his ribs and feeling the softness as I split his heart. The surprise in his eyes as his soul fled his body was enough signal for me to guide my horse away as he fell leaving his sword in my shield. As predicted, the seething venom of his woman screamed its hatred as the heavy oaf fell to the slimy turf. Her fast black mare spun towards me and she vented her wrath with sword and tongue, flailing like a mad-woman.

I almost felt pity as our swords met, realising her strength was almost spent in voicing her grief, and in that seconds' distraction she lunged, slicing my mare's shoulder and neck. The mare screamed and I saw a flash of white in her eye as she swung her neck in disbelief at her wound. My anger flared red as I called on the killing power of the Morrigan to back me as I slayed my friend's attacker.

The weak man was a surprise. He stood back watching, giving the woman space for her revenge. Then rested, he rejoined her battle and ploughed into us with steady thoughtful swordsmanship. He was strong and fast, his skill at recovery and changing positions caught me a couple of times. The nicks he inflicted on my arms only served to fuel my hatred and as I observed my mare's courage to continue with a gaping wound my second wind offered me renewed speed and strength. Focussed only on the battle in front of me, no sound edged into my arena as I aimed low slicing his thigh deeply with my honed blade. He flinched and dropped his guard grasping his leg long enough for my shield to meet his face. The boss met his nose and cheek, splintering bone - the cumbersome passenger sword cut into his chest and face - obviously confusing him as to its presence there. A second strike from my grandmother's sword sprayed blood from his jugular and I heard her ghostly cackle above me as her spirit viewed our victory with pride.

The battle round me had fizzled out. The remaining standing warriors had reduced to sword-on-sword clunks and grunts, all strength and anger spent and only determination driving them. I could go in and fell them or leave the field now with pride and nurse my horse. I thanked my spirit guardians and watched as they left the battlefield like ghostly ravens.

With the immediate danger over I felt the mare's head drop a little and saw her nostrils flare - suddenly she felt the pain - it was time to leave.

I cantered gently past the bodies of the slain, now feeling

heavy and sick with post-fight fatigue and headed for the healers in our camp. The battle was over - even out-numbered we had held the ground and still had many living but badly wounded warriors. We had won! But no elation - my mare was wounded.

I fell off the back of the horse into the arms of a woman who helped me to the ground and offered me the sweetest coldest water I have ever tasted. "The horse, see to the horse" I choked. "It is done" she replied as skilled hands cleaned and dressed her wound with a thick blood-stemming paste. Her mouth was sponged with water and as she was nursed and soothed I sank into the depths of velvet black sleep and prepared my mind for another day...

Onward

This morning I look at the catkins hanging on the hazel, as the mist clears the tops of the trees down the valley. The bees have come out in the sunshine, hungry to find early sources of pollen. My bin-bag crows are calling from the tops of the oaks, still naked of leaves, where they are constructing their stick nests. The nests always make me think of my grandson's 'Kerplunck' game where you try to remove as many sticks as possible before the marble plunks down through the construction. I imagine the little eggs balanced there in trepidation awaiting the fall. But judging by the marauding hordes in my chicken-run, many seem to make it.

And so another season begins as the land awakens and the sun warms the ground that is waiting for my young plants which are sprouting in my greenhouse - the cycle continues. Uncle Math would have finished cutting his hedge by now - he always had it done before March came in. Campbell would have finished ploughing if the weather was right and would be ready to seed the fields.

Always hurrying but never rushing, the jobs were driven by the weather. I explain all this to my youngest daughter who is mildly interested in what I'm planting and she smiles at me with that sympathetic look that says 'silly old fart - what is she going on about?'. But I hope one day she will remember and tell the same stories to her daughters.

Endings and new beginnings, the human cycle continues too, and I wish for the ability to inject the old wisdoms into the young heads so one day they will be able to appreciate the beauty of blackbird song. I do not feel ready to be the elder yet - I would like to go back to my childhood with my current understanding and do it again so I can glean more knowledge and information from the old ones. However, ageing I am, and I hope to wear that mantle with honour and dignity like my elders have done before me and enjoy the gifts it brings. Suddenly I struggle to think what they might be ... ... a weak bladder, too much weight round the middle, an arthritic ankle and failing sight ... Oh bloody hell. Only last week I felt really daft when I whipped my specs off and dropped them on the floor, forgetting they were the ones without the 'old fart string' round my neck. Stepping forward to pick them up, I trod on them, rendering them suitable to fit a Picasso portrait - much to the amusement of my patient who watched this farce. Right then I thought that Harry Potter's 'Reparo' charm might be useful after all!

But my Dad told me "Trouble comes to every door - it's how you handle it that makes you a prince or a pauper". Magic is not an instant cure for trouble, a guarantee for trouble-free bliss or even an alternative lifestyle. It is an extra dimension that can be overlaid on everyday life, interwoven and discovered at any turn your life takes.

Amidst the bin-bag crows is a young one with white patches. Apparently accepted, she fights for recognition like the other youngsters and looks for her place in the pecking order. My attention is drawn to a mobbing above as a hawk glides on the thermals and the crows cackle behind with undignified verbals. Untiring they keep up the haranguing, flapping and worrying until the hawk lazily moves on. I look back down and in front of me I gaze in wonder - am I truly seeing this? - on the fence of the paddock sit five crows, on the fence of the chicken-run opposite sit three magpies and on the ground between them is my black-and-white crow. She is looking from one group to the other as if asking where she belongs. So often have I felt the same! I watch her deliberation with curiosity and sympathy as she walks along the path with both sides calling to her. I stand up yelling "Go on wee bird - stand in your own space, don't listen to them". I continue "You are beautiful as you are - fly high!" The crows look at me, unmoved by my outburst. The sun glares brighter as I stare into it to see what the pied crow does. Squinting, I look up toward the path, my eyes watering from the brightness and my feelings for this court. I wipe my eyes and when I look up, there in front of me is a shimmering image of a beautiful black and silver-haired woman. A glow surrounds her black robes and her blue eyes pierce me. "You show me care, child of the Earth". I bow my head in reverence and slight disbelief. Glancing back up I see her still there - no it's not my imagination. I wonder can this be the Morrigan? She is too beautiful and kinder than I know. She laughs gently - "I take many shapes and forms, Earth child, but you recognise me well - keep care of this land and her life, and you will be rewarded."

I raise my head to ask a question and the crows take off in one startling flap, clouds of them rising up from the chicken run ... and she's gone.

I smile and inhale deeply as the warm sense of recognition and knowing flows through my body. I look round me at the fields and the hedges and I know their potential - the future is a journey I can't wait to embark on...

...The mystery continues.

Gifts for your Path

Thank you for travelling through my story with me.

Let me now offer you some exercises and contemplations to assist you on your journey.

Each offering ties in loosely with the chapters and will help you to tune in to the energies of the inner planes. The poems are words that sing to me, may they also inspire you.

Journey to Find Your Soul Purpose

If you are not already familiar with your soul self, your soul family or your soul group and you wish to meet them, or if you are familiar with them and wish to work with them in some way, then this is a journey that will help you achieve this.

First find a quiet safe place where you will not be disturbed. Draw a circle, either physical or energetic, and mark the four quarters within it. Move and sit in the west, the place of the ancestors, which holds the qualities of the emotional self. Take three deep breaths, in through your nose, out through your mouth, which will help you to concentrate and steady your breath. Either drumming, humming or breathing, to drop your awareness to a trancelike state, let the rhythm carry you down to your deepest level.

In your mind's eye, visualise a landscape - it may be a place you already know, or a place of your imagination - it could be a woodland, stone circle, round house, your own garden or room. Look round and familiarise yourself with this landscape. In the centre of the area you see a person standing there, when you look closely you see that person is you. It may not look like you now, but you know in your heart that it is you. This is your soul self.

Look more closely and observe what you are wearing - can you gauge a time period or place where you may be? Can you recognise any of your facial features as resembling any of your ancestors or family members? Really watch yourself and try to get a sense of this person - are you old or young, strong or weak, healthy or sick, wise or dull?

When you feel ready, introduce yourself to your soul self. This may feel a strange or difficult - or silly - thing to do, but go with it if you can. Just tell them your name as it is now and say the time you are living in and request that they introduce you to more of your soul family or group. They may, or may not, tell you their name. If they do, this is a name you should never share with anyone else. Names have power.

You are led to a doorway or gateway in keeping with your surroundings and as you pass through you see a line of people stretching away into the distance. In the front of the line, the people are dressed in the clothing of today. As it stretches away from you, the clothing shows the line going back in time. Your soul self leads back along this line of people and as you go you see faces you recognise, some may be family members or close friends and as you go back in time you may see some faces you recognise from dreams or visions. Some are familiar and friendly and some may make you feel uncomfortable for some reason.

All these beings are souls that you have had some connection to in past life or lives. They are relevant to your life now and some you may wish to talk to and ask questions of, others you may wish to come back and meet again. Any beings that make you feel uncomfortable may be able to help you work through traumas you are currently dealing with, so do try to speak to them to find out what the connection is and why you find their presence difficult.

When you feel ready to return, or your soul self guides you to return, thank your soul group for their time and information and allow yourself to be guided back through your doorway or gateway to your familiar landscape. Thank your soul self for being your guide and helping you on this journey. Go back to your place in the west and settle back into your rhythmic breathing, humming or drumming, and as you do so, feel yourself return to your circle and become aware of your surroundings. Slowly open your eyes and when you feel rooted back in your physical space, stop and take three deep breaths. Stand up and give yourself a good shake, then go and write anything down that you may wish to remember from this journey. Have something nice to eat and drink to ground yourself back in the here and now.

Grounding Exercise

This is a wonderful grounding exercise but requires concentration and good visualisation. For many people it can be quite confusing at first, but persevere if you can because it is worth it. If needs be, use a diagram or draw a diagram that you can understand to follow as you do it.

We will be working with the seven chakra system.

Find a quiet place where you will not be disturbed or distracted. Sit, preferably on an upright chair with your feet planted flat on the floor. This is better than lying down as you are less likely to fall asleep. Breathe in through your nose and out through your mouth, with really big breaths, close your eyes and settle into a relaxed breathing pattern. Focus on your breath as it enters and leaves your body and gradually be aware as it slows down and you sink into a slightly deeper level of awareness. The sounds of the outside world are no longer within your realm of being.

Starting with your base chakra, which is associated with a deep blood red colour, imagine each energy centre as a vessel of some shape or form. This may range from a jug to a tank to a room-sized shape that you can fill or empty of the liquid colour of each chakra. I visualise a jug, but you can visualise whatever comes easiest to the picture in your mind. When you have a clear vision in your mind's eye - watch the deep red liquid flow out of the vessel on each out-breath, see it flow down your legs, through your feet, on down through the floor, further down through the surfaces of the Earth to a deep lake of crimson red. Watch it all flow down until your chakra is empty. This may take several breaths before you feel ready to move on to the next centre.

Repeat the same process with bright orange in the sacral chakra, watching as it travels through the base chakra of red, and on down through the Earth. When it reaches the lake of red, see it travel all the way through it, deeper toward the centre of the Earth, until it reaches a lake of orange, then watch as the chakra vessel empties into the lake.

Continue with the yellow of the solar plexus, green of the heart chakra, bright electric blue of the throat chakra, indigo of the third eye centre, and purple of the crown chakra. Use the same process of visualising each colour pour out of the jug of the chakra area and down your legs through the previous energy centre and lake of colour, as you work towards the centre of the Earth. When all the chakras are empty, begin the process of drawing up.

Beginning again with deep red, draw the colour up from this red lake, now energised and replenished, and with each in-breath watch as it travels up through the surface of the Earth, the floor of your room, your feet, legs and then into your base chakra. Watch as the base chakra fills to capacity and beginning to overflow with this beautiful red liquid energy. Again repeat the same process with an in-breath drawing up each of the colours, with orange, yellow, green, blue, indigo, and purple until each chakra centre is replenished and balanced.

Then view yourself sitting in your chair with the colours of each chakra glowing and the energy swirling. See a thread of red connecting you deep to the centre of the Earth and a thread of purple connecting you up to the Universe. Then as you watch see the colours swirl and mingle, creating a mix of colour above, below, round and through you. See the mixed colour form into an egg-shape with the base of it buried into the ground, connecting it to the Earth.

Now you will feel different - your energy is grounded and each chakra in balance - a feeling of deep peace and contentment flows through you.

This is an exercise to practice regularly before or after doing any energy work or if you have experienced a time of stress. The more you do it, the easier it becomes, and you will soon be able to do it as quickly or slowly as you choose.

Discovering the Path

In this chapter we examine death, a thing so often marginalised. Here my mother-in-law's poem captures the sentiments of many who may not have a voice to speak in their time of passing.

Rita's Poem

Wait with me please
in the hour of my death.
Do not deny me time
or hasten me into loneliness.
If you can be willing to be there
we will hold hands and wait together
as I would hold your hand and wait with you,
content to let the last quiet hours pass.
Neither to force them on
or try to hold them back.
When the sun touches the rim of the world
it does not take so very long to set.
When I sat waiting at my father's side
I held his hand and smiled at him until
his hand had changed and I knew that he had died.
So also, as I die, please wait a moment more
after all breath has gone,
then you shall see, as I there gladly saw,
the liberating mystery.

Rita Simon 1976

Losing the Path

This poem sat with me as I saw many of my dreams being trampled over.

It became my mantra.

As my Dad would say: "Bonny words".

Aedh Wishes for the Cloths of Heaven

Had I the heavens' embroidered cloths,
Enwrought with golden and silver light,
The blue and the dim and the dark cloths
Of night and light and the half-light,
I would spread the cloths under your feet:
But I, being poor, have only my dreams;
I have spread my dreams under your feet;
Tread softly because you tread on my dreams.

William Butler Yeats (1865-1939)

Moon Magic Charm

This is a charm that you can use to end a relationship or situation and is performed during a waning moon. Her influence on your magic now is that of decreasing. In the last quarter the moon generally rises at midnight and sets at noon, and is visible from the second half of the night to early morning. It is essential to perform your magic when you can see the moon and it is not overcast, and so it must be done between midnight and five am, when the moon is still visible in the sky. When both the sun and moon can be seen do not work moon magic then as sun energy is strong and will influence the more subtle energy of the moon.

Light a white or pale blue candle which is new and will only be used during this ritual. Begin by bathing in a hot bath with a few drops of rose essence in the water. As you soak, cleanse yourself of all negative thought and prepare yourself to begin your spell. With an open mind emptied of all distraction, think through your intentions and form clear concise invocations in your mind, choosing your words carefully.

Go outside under the moon and find a quiet place where you will not be disturbed. Place your candle where it won't blow out. Put a bowl of water where it will catch the reflections of the moon. Then anoint your forehead with some rose essence or blessed moon essence (even better if it has been sitting in the moonlight for a while first) while looking at the crescent moon speak your intention clearly, stating that you want to end the relationship or situation. Ask that this happens with gentleness and care and with love. Ask for guidance on how to do this effectively and then gaze into your bowl of water. Let your focus blur and breathe deeply, letting your awareness drop into a trance-like state. As you continue to watch Her reflection, be aware of any pictures or instructions that come into your consciousness. Be guided by your thoughts. When you feel you have done enough, let your awareness of your *surroundings return and whilst looking at the crone moon, thank her for her wisdom and guidance. Lift your bowl and drink some of the water to imbibe her instruction, then as you pour away the remaining water see yourself pouring away your situation and visualise the water going through the water cycle and carrying your thoughts and words out into the World.*

Repeat this ritual during the last quarter until two days before dark moon, unless it is something so serious that you wish to bring it to a complete end. In this dark night you are completely unprotected by Her gentling light and so the banishing forces are very strong. Use this time with care and only if all else has failed.

Give it a whole moon cycle to work and by this time next moon you should see changes starting to happen.

A Changing World

Mother Earth needs our assistance, may we be as generous with her as she is with us.

Be Green

Put your mind to it and you will find that changing one thing per week in your life is a hardly noticeable effort, but in one year's time you will have made a difference to Mother Earth. Here are well over 52 examples for you to choose from. Do them in any order that inspires you, research and improve them, substitute something of your own, and enjoy the journey to a better world.

Generally, all these suggestions will help conserve energy and resources for humanity's future. All of them will save you time and money as well, and some will bring you nicer sights, sounds, tastes and smells, too! I've not explained them in detail - if you want to know more, start researching!

1. *Reduce your electricity consumption - change to energy efficient light bulbs, turn off and unplug as many room lights and standby lights as you can.*
2. *Reduce your water consumption - half-fill your kettle, switch the tap off when you brush your teeth, put lids on saucepans, get rid of the dishwasher, share a bath, only flush the toilet for a poo, re-use greywater for your hedges and trees.*
3. *Reduce your gas consumption - turn the heating thermostat down, put foil behind your radiators, only heat the rooms you use, upgrade your boiler, use a multi-fuel stove.*
4. *Insulate your home - your wall cavity, your loft and your windows (install double or triple glazing) - if you have older brick buildings seek out council grants and insulation company deals.*
5. *Use less petrol - go by bus or train, ride a bike, join a car-share scheme, work at home if possible.*

6   Explore alternative energy sources - wind-powered, solar-powered, water-powered, ground or air-source, photo voltaic-electric, etc.

7.   Re-cycle your compostable waste - all uncooked food from the kitchen, newspapers and brown cardboard, lawn clippings.

8.   Recycle as much as you can - paper, glass bottles, tin cans, mobile phones and clothes.

9.   Save trees - save paper for scrap notes, re-use envelopes, read & delete emails rather than print them, use email rather than faxes.

10.   Review your food-habits - go vegetarian once a week, grow your own food (and use your compost), use perishables while they're fresh.

11.   Re-arrange your washing habits - wait for a full washing machine load, hang your clothes outside to dry, use a cool wash.

12.   Reduce your use of disposable plastics - avoid bottled water, re-use old plastic bags, buy food loose instead of plastic wrapped, use matches instead of disposable lighters.

13.   Reduce your use of chemicals - use cut flowers instead of air-fresheners, use less bleach etc., use environmentally friendly washing powders, use hand-weeding and weed-control designs instead of weed-killers.

14.   Reduce your use of pharmaceuticals - return un-used drugs to chemists, eat organic foods, stop smoking, eat more honey, try natural medicines and therapies.

15.   Reorganise your food shopping - reduce the number of trips by bulk shopping, buy fresh foods for new recipes, buy local food to save food-miles.

16.   Join a like-minded eco-group in your area (or virtually) - explore Freecycle.com, find a permaculture group, volunteer for an eco-charity, use charity shops more thoughtfully, add your voice to groups like Transition Towns, Parallel Community, Amnesty International, Friends of the Earth, etc.

Words have Power

Meg showed dignity in her decision to move on. I hope the Grey Mare story shows you there can be joy in transition.

The Grey Mare

Untethered, the grey mare galloped across the wild moor, tossing her head and allowing the wind to blow through her mane. She kicked up her heels and felt her tail fly free. On she ran her body lithe and light, galloping faster and faster, losing all trace of thought or care or memory of what had gone before. Her heart beat faster as she ran and so she ran faster to the sound of her own drum. Her lungs tightened as her nostrils flared but now she could not stop, she could only go faster, sucked into the momentum of the journey. Her dark brown eyes looked to the sun and she flew towards the light her weight felt less and the effort to run seemed easier. Suddenly her feet left the ground and she was truly flying. Free of burden, free of life, she continued in spirit and knew then that death is the gift and living the hard part. At last she had found peace.

Mhairi Simon

Practice your Skills as a Caller

If you fancy trying your skills as a caller start with something easy. Find a place where you can meditate and move into a trance state having first decided who you are going to call. It's too easy to choose the family dog who may only be five feet away from you. Instead aim for a wild animal but not something too rare, like a panda if you live in the middle of Birmingham! Equally you don't want to focus on something like a pigeon who may be round you anyway. Perhaps choose a fox or a barn owl, or a dolphin or a porpoise if you live by the sea. It's best to have an understanding of the animal you decide to call so that you don't pull it out of its normal routine too much.

When you are ready to begin and your focus has dropped to trance-state, picture your animal in your mind's eye. Hold the vision and introduce yourself then ask if you can have audience, if it will come to you or if you can visit it. Await your reply. If you need to go to it to guide it to you then allow your astral body to leave your physical body and travel to your animal friend. Connect with it and allow your mind to contact hers and ask her if she is willing to follow you home.

Take some time to observe her movement and try to understand her thinking. Travel with her and watch where she goes and what she is doing. Encourage her to let you guide her to you and travel back to your body. Be sure at this point to make yourself re-enter your physical body. When your breathing has settled back to its usual rhythm, come back to your awakened state and look round for your friend - has she come? Enjoy your time with her and then thank her for allowing you contact and for her time and release your connection with her to let her go on in safety. If not successful this time, try again another day - practice makes perfect!

Treat Each of Your Senses

To lift your spirits, treat each of the senses to something special. Close your eyes and imagine what the most wonderful thing in the world would be for you to see, hear, touch, taste, smell and for your sixth sense to experience.

Sight:- ask yourself what appeals to your eyes and indulge them in a wonderful vision. Look at a beautiful picture or get up early to watch the sunrise. Give the eyes themselves a treat too, use euphrasia eyewash then lie quietly with some camomile eyepads to make them feel nice.

Sound:- what do you like to hear? Is it birdsong or sweet music, or silence? Give your ears a treat and take them to a place where you can only hear what you want to. Blot out all background babble, hum or traffic noise, stay away from phones and just enjoy some time listening to what appeals to your ears.

Touch:- touch is not only about being touched but about touching as well. First treat your body to a relaxing bubbly bath and consider getting a massage where your skin is soothed and pampered. An Indian head-massage can transport you to a relaxed happy place. Perhaps you prefer giving one which appeals to your sense of touch or run your fingers through your lover's hair, your dogs coat or over a silky piece of clothing. Maybe you prefer to make pastry where your fingers can squish dough. Think what feels nice to you.

Taste:- Indulge your tastebuds today. Find the most wonderful food and drink treats and eat them. Or search out something unusual that you have never tasted before and be adventurous.

Smell:- Start your day with incense that makes you feel good and relaxed. Go to a flower shop and sniff some flowers. Smell a new perfume that appeals to you. Or your thing may be clean sheets on the bed or coming home to the smell of baking. Freshly cut grass is a smell that lingers in your brain - does it lift your mood and make you think of summer?

Sixth sense:- lie in a relaxed place and allow your consciousness to drop into that trance-like space and let your mind go blank. Remain in that neutral place and whenever you find you are drawn into the thinking process focus back on your breath and guide your mind back into neutral. Things may come through for you to witness, but refuse to act on anything, just keep going back to a place of no mind and give your sixth sense a thorough rest.

These are just suggestions to guide you toward things that may stimulate the senses. Use your imagination to explore more ideas that will appeal to you.

Now take a deep breath...

...and begin!

Glossary of Old Scottish words

burn	a small stream
byre	a shed where cattle are kept
Cailleach	crone aspect of the Goddess of the Land
Cernunos	Horned God
Drui-en	the wren, King of Birds
dykes	dry stone walls
guising	dressing in disguise for fun, usually referring to Samhain celebrations
howf	an unkempt house
keek	a surreptitious peek
midden	muck heap
quagmire	muddy watery bog
Sidhe	the Shining Ones
skelped	smacked
smir	a fine grey misty rain
strapping	slapping technique used to tone the muscles
spyugs	baby birds, not yet fledged
tumshie	turnip
wisp	a plait of straw used for grooming a horse (wisping) to increase circulation

Suggested Reading List

Hamish Miller: Sun & Serpent: An Investigation into Earth Energies, with Paul Broadhurst, Pendragon Press, 1989, ISBN 0951518313

Bill Mollison: Permaculture One: A Perennial Agriculture for Human Settlements, with David Holmgren, Trasworld Publishers, 1978, ISBN 978-0938240006

Rob Hopkins: The Transition Handbook, ISBN 978 1 900322 18 8, NOW ONLY AVAILABLE AS AN E-BOOK

Masaru Emoto: Messages from Water, Vol. 1 (June 1999), Hado Publishing, ISBN 4-939098-00-1

Rev.John Gregorson Campbell: The Gaelic Otherworld: Rev.John Gregorson Campbell's Superstitions of the Highlands and the Islands of Scotland and Witchcraft and Second Sight in the Highlands and Islands, Birlinn Ltd; illustrated edition (1 May 2008)   ISBN-13: 978-1841587332